The Burton Court Recipes

The Burton Court Recipes

English food from Herefordshire

by
Helen J Simpson

Logaston Press
1991

LOGASTON PRESS
Little Logaston Woonton Almeley
Herefordshire HR3 6QH

First published by Logaston Press 1991
Copyright © Text Helen J Simpson
Copyright © Photographs Benjamin Corbett
Copyright © Drawings Ken Hutchinson

ISBN 1 873827 00 8

Set in Baskerville 10/13 pt by Logaston Press
and printed in Great Britain by Ebenezer Baylis & Son
Worcester

Cover photo: Clockwise from the left: Apple & Blackberry Tansy,
Jenny's Raspberry Creams, Tayberry Whip, Orange & Ginger Cream,
Marigold Flan, Velvet or Hedgehog Pudding

For Robert and my sons Henry and Edward
also to the memory of Julia 'Dickens' Lewin

Acknowledgments

I have many people to thank for their help in the final production of this book. First it would never have been written without the generous advice and knowledge imparted to me by the publisher Ann Haly who reproduces historic cookery books. She pointed me in the direction of where to research into this country's cookery covering the seven centuries of Burton Court's existence. In the end I have barely skimmed the surface, to go deeper would perhaps be best left to the official food historians. But I owe Ann a tremendous debt.

I also wish to acknowledge the invaluable help given to me by the following: cousins Frances Atkinson and Christine Cocks, the American master baker Bernard Clayton Jr. and his wife Margery, Alice Klouda, Patrick Morton, Castle Ashby archivist Peter McKay, Home Economist Ann Searle, Mrs E. Smith for the Burton Court staff records, Elizabeth Ray, Thomas Stock, the Hon. Mrs Diana Uhlman, Margaret West and Clarissa Dickson Wright. Also the Literary Trustees of Walter de la Mare and the Society of Authors as their representative for permission to reproduce *I Can't Abear*, the photographer Benjamin Corbett, Peter Manders for the illustration on page 69, Ken Hutchinson for all the other illustrations and finally to my publishers Andy Johnson and Steve Punter of Logaston Press.

Contents

We may live without poetry, music and art,
We may live without conscience, and live without heart,
We may live without friends, we may live without books,
But civilised man cannot live without cooks.

He may live without books—what is knowledge but grieving?
He may live without hope—what is hope but deceiving?
He may live without love—what is passed on but pining?
But where is the man that can live without dining?

Owen Meredith
(Sent to the editor, London *Daily Chronicle*, 12 December 1911)

Introduction

For the past nineteen years I have been cooking some thousands of scone teas for strangers, and on the more creative side introducing small parties of overseas visitors to the delights of English and especially Herefordshire cookery.

The emphasis has been on home produced food with the soft-fruits from Burton Court's own farm, as the flavours of English fruit are special. A Herefordshire cox's apple or English peach or nectarine is unsurpassed. Vegetables from the kitchen garden are used, together with fresh salmon from the River Wye, beef from the world famous Hereford cattle and lamb from the Welsh and border flocks, whilst Herefordshire cider is often used.

Though I am a true Herefordian by birth, earlier generations were not. My great-grandmother married a tenant farmer on the Marquis of Northampton's estate at Castle Ashby, kept a farm guesthouse and from all accounts was a renowned cook. It is not surprising that some of these recipes were handed down through the family and I have included a selection in this book. Others are entirely my own invention and I do hope you will enjoy trying them for yourself.

At Burton Court we have a collection of costumes through the centuries, and I must confess that every year as I mount and display the costume exhibition I contemplate what their owners would have eaten whilst wearing their apparel!

However, what follows is a culinary journey through the whole period of Burton Court's existence, from the area's earliest settlers, to the visit of Henry V in 1402, through its Victorian heyday when no fewer than 23 servants were employed. The servants' bells, restored by my husband, still ring, but there is no-one now to answer them. Some of the old retainers are still alive, and in their eighties have told us stories of the 'upstairs and downstairs' life at the Court, some of them related in the chapter on Victorian cooking.

With history and food entwined, happy reading, and happy cooking!

Helen J. Simpson
September 1991

Early Days to the Fourteenth Century

Because the site of Burton Court is on that of an ancient British camp, people have probably lived here for over 2,000 years. However, the name is derived from the Saxon words Burh and Ton, meaning a fortified dwelling place.

The surviving rolls of the manor begin in the reign of Edward III, in 1331. No mention is made of its lord until 1402, when the name of Thomas St. Owen is recorded. The Great Hall dates from the Fourteenth Century and is believed to have had a central fireplace. The seventy feet deep mediaeval well still exists in the cellars.

In noble households the mediaeval cook was always a man—he was highly skilled and well paid, attended usually by numerous scullions. People in the Middle Ages loved brightly coloured foods, but the cooks' colouring agents were limited. They used saffron for yellow, herbs to obtain green and sandalwood chips were stewed in water to produce a red liquid.

The cook initially owed much to the legacy of the Romans who introduced pheasants, peacocks, guinea fowl and fallow deer into Britain. They also cultivated vines, fig, walnut, medlar, mulberry and chestnut trees, as well as introducing herbs such as parsley, coriander, fennel, mint, thyme, garlic and sage, whilst importing dates, olives, olive oil, pepper, ginger and cinnamon, all valued in their diet.

The cook next benefited from the Crusades which saw an important change in English cooking. Due to lack of winter feeds many cattle had to be killed in the autumn and the meat somehow kept until the following spring, by which time it was barely tolerable to the nose or palate. But the Crusaders brought back supplies of spices enabling the meat to become quite presentable.

The accomplished mediaeval cook used these spices as well as a wide variety of herbs such as anise, borage (which was thought to revive the hypochondriac and cheer the hard student!), burnet, clary, good King Henry (which is rich in iron), lovage, hyssop, purslane, rocket, summer savory, sorrel and tansy with its scent of ginger. There was also parsley, sage, garlic, rosemary, mint, watercress, fennel and rue.

The following recipes do likewise.

Creamed Nettle Purée

Prehistoric Britons lived on the wild vegetation. Many plants were collected and cooked; nettles were boiled, made into soups and sometimes the juice was combined with Lady's Bedstraw and used in rennet form in making cheese.

Nettles have a reputation as a wonderful blood cleanser and tonic. They are richer in iron than spinach, contain more protein than cabbage and more vitamins than many other green vegetables. As for taste, they are similar to spinach.

Ingredients (Serves 4)
Appx. 225g or half a lb nettle leaves
2 tbs green spring onion or shallot tops
1 clove garlic, finely sliced
Salt & freshly ground pepper
2 tbs single cream

Method
Wearing gloves pick the first four or five leaves at the top of the nettle stem (not the green tassel-like flowers) when they are starting to sprout in the spring. The larger leaves below tend to be too bitter.

Wash and cook the leaves in a liberal amount of fast-boiling water, which tends to help retain the vitamins, adding the onion tops, garlic, salt and pepper.

Drain well (the water can be kept for soup) and chop finely then add the cream. Serve immediately. Can be served with sticks of mixed hot vegetables, such as carrots, parsnips, asparagus and celery.

Erbowle (Damsons in red wine and honey)

Ingredients (Serves 4)
675 kg or 1 and a half lbs stoned damsons
450 ml or three-quarters pint of red wine
4 tbs honey
Half tsp powderfort (a mixture of ground dried chives and mace)
85 g or 3 oz rice flour
Anise

Method
Stew the damsons in the wine until they are soft and pass them through a strainer or liquidizer (having removed the stones!).

Replace the purée in the wine and add the honey, powderfort and rice flour and simmer until the mixture thickens, adding more rice flour if necessary.

Serve garnished with leaves and flowers of anise.

Roast Wood Pigeons in a Roman Sauce

'Pygeons be easily dygested and very holsome to them whiche are fleumatike or pure melancholy.' Sir Thomas Elyot, *A castel of Helthe* 1539

In Roman Britain wood pigeons were a major source of meat, the Romans building pigeon-houses, or columbaria, where pigeons could nest and breed. The sauce recipe comes from the world's oldest cookery book, written in the first century under the name of Celius Apicius, a rich epicure who lived in Rome, and of which thirty-two manuscript excerpts survived down to the fifth century. The Romans used honey widely, especially in their sauces, and this sauce recipe was updated and selected by Jane Renfrew in her book *Food and Cooking in Roman Britain - History and Recipes*.

Ingredients (Serves 4)
2 tender young pigeons
55g or 2 oz butter
Pepper & salt
115g or 4 oz fat salt pork or bacon, thinly sliced
2 slices white bread for toast

For the Roman sauce
A pinch of each of pepper, lovage, fresh coriander,
    mint and dried onion
100g or 4 oz stoned dates
1 egg yolk
15ml or 1 tbs wine
15ml or 1 tbs vinegar
15ml or 1 tbs olive oil
15ml or 1 tbs honey
5ml or 1 tsp anchovy essence
Watercress to garnish

Method
Sprinkle the inside of the birds with salt and pepper and put a large knob of butter inside the birds to keep them moist whilst cooking. Truss them up tidily and spread with butter. Bard (or wrap) the birds with strips of fat salt pork or bacon. Place them on a piece of toast in a roasting tin.

Cook the birds in a hot oven, 425°F, 210°C, gas mark 7, for 20 minutes per lb., basting frequently during cooking. Remove the fat strips for the last 10 to 15 minutes. Sprinkle the breasts lightly with flour and continue cooking until brown. Keep warm.

Prepare the sauce. Pound the pepper, herbs and onion together in a mortar. Add the dates and egg yolk and stir until smooth.

Mix the remaining ingredients in a pan, add the mixture from the mortar, and heat gently until the sauce thickens, stirring all the time.

Cut the pigeons in half, and pour the sauce over them. Garnish with watercress.

King Offa's Paté

King Offa, King of Mercia in the eighth century, constructed a massive earthwork which ran much of the way from Flintshire in North Wales down through Herefordshire to the River Severn in Gloucestershire. The dyke, named after him, lies not many miles from Burton Court and marked the western limit of Anglo-Saxon power.

This paté was inspired by the introduction of the first cider brandy to this country after a gap of some 200 years. Bertram Bulmer, former chairman of Bulmer's in Hereford, opened a cider museum in the city, and King Offa Cider Brandy was also largely his creation.

Ingredients
350g or 12 ozs unsalted belly pork
55g or 2 ozs lard
1 medium sliced onion
3 crushed garlic cloves
225g or 8 ozs bacon pieces
225g or 8 ozs pigs liver
450g or 1 lb chicken livers
1 egg
Half tsp ground mace
1 level tbs chopped fresh herbs
    (parsley, thyme or basil or tarragon)
Quarter tsp salt and ground black pepper
4 tbs King Offa Cider Brandy
30g or 1 oz semolina or ground rice
285g or 10 ozs streaky bacon rashers derinded
1 or 2 bay leaves

Method
Skin and bone the belly pork.

Put lard, onion and garlic in a pan, cover and fry till soft.

Mince pork, bacon pieces, liver, onion and garlic.

Add the rest of the ingredients, except the bacon rashers, including 2 of the tablespoons of cider brandy to the minced mixture, and mix well together.

Stretch the bacon with the back of a knife and line the inside of a 3 pint terrine or dish.

Pour the mixture into the dish. Place a bay leaf or two on the top. Cover with grease-proof paper and foil.

Place in a bain-marie (or large pan), and half fill with boiling water as a water bath.

Bake at 325°F, 170°C, gas mark 3 for about 2 hours 30 minutes.

Remove from the water bath. Place a double thickness of foil on top of the cooked paté, removing the lid if used, and weigh down with weights.

Leave to cool and chill overnight. Remove weights, then trim surplus bacon around the edge, turn out, and inject a further 2 tablespoons of cider brandy into the paté with a skewer or clean knitting needle.

Loyne of Pork with Sorrel Sauce

Taken from *The Forme of Cury*, a roll of ancient English cookery compiled about 1390 by the master cooks of King Richard II. This recipe used to be called Cormarye, and a note explains that 'The Lyne of the Pork, is fro the hippe boon to the hede'. The sorrel sauce makes a change from apple sauce.

Florence White, founder of the English Folk Cookery Association in 1931, said that 'in Herefordshire farmhouses a piece of fresh pork (if available) is roasted and served with roast chicken.'

Ingredients (Serves 6)
1.35kg or 3lb loin of pork
2 cloves garlic
1 tsp ground coriander seeds
1 tsp ground caraway seeds
1 tsp freshly ground black pepper
150ml or quarter pint of red wine
2 tsp salt

For the sorrel sauce
Appx. 450g or 1 lb sorrel leaves
45g or 1 and a half oz butter
150ml or quarter pint single cream
Salt & pepper to taste

Method
Score the pork in narrow lines.

Crush the garlic and mix it with the coriander, caraway, pepper, salt and wine.

Rub some of the mixture well into the meat, wrap it in cooking foil but before closing, pour the rest of the mixture over the joint.

Place in a roasting dish and roast in a hot oven, 425°F, 220°C, gas mark 7, for 10 minutes and then reduce the heat for the remainder of the cooking time to 350°F, 180°C, gas mark 4. Cook for 1 hour 40 minutes. Open the foil for the last half hour of the cooking to allow the crackling to crisp.

Keep the meat hot and make a gravy using the sediment which remains in the dish.

Meanwhile prepare the sorrel sauce. Wash the sorrel leaves, chop coarsely and fry lightly in the butter with salt and pepper until tender. Remove from the heat and allow to cool slightly. Stir in the cream. Reheat gently and serve.

Herefordshire Eel in a Herb Sauce

In *The Forme of Cury* written in 1378, the recipe says 'Take the conger and fcald hym, and fmte hym in pecys, and feeth hym. Take parfel (parsley), mynt, peletes (pellitory), rofmarye, and a litul fawge, rede and falt, powdor-fort, and a litel garlec, clowes (cloves) a lit; take and grynd it wel. Drawe (strain) it up with vynegar thrugh a cloth. Caft the fyfshe in a veffel, and caft the fewe (liquor) onoward, and ferve it forth.'

The method given below was updated by Maxime McKendry in her book *Seven Hundred years of English Cooking*.

Ingredients (Serves 2 to 3)

1 eel, skinned
575ml or 1 pint fish stock
4 tbs parsley
2 tbs mint
1 tsp rosemary
Half tsp sage
2 cloves of garlic, crushed
30g or 1 oz breadcrumbs
Half tsp salt
Powderfort (2 tbs chives chopped
    with half tsp powdered mace)
4 cloves, crushed
4 tbs vinegar

Method

Skin the eel, cut it into slices and simmer in the fish stock, using the skin for flavour, until tender.

Chop together the parsley, mint, rosemary and sage. Put in a blender with the crushed garlic, the breadcrumbs, salt, powderfort and crushed cloves. Add a little vinegar and blend well. Rub through a sieve, using a little more vinegar to wash the mixture through.

Arrange the eel slices in a fireproof dish, pour the sauce over them and reheat, spooning the sauce over the fish from time to time so that it can absorb the flavour.

Simmer for between 10 and 15 minutes and serve.

Leek Pottage

This especially popular soup in mediaeval Britain was known as Leek Pottage or White Porray. Various kinds of roots from the garden were added such as carrots, turnips and rapes. When a thicker soup was required a thickening agent such as ground almonds, though affordable only to the rich, were used. I've included potatoes, though these weren't introduced into Britain until 1580.

Ingredients (Serves 4 to 5)
450g or 1 lb leeks
55g or 2 oz butter
1 large red potato
575ml or 1 scant pint chicken stock
1 bay leaf
1 tsp salt
575 ml or 1 scant pint milk
A little cornflour to thicken soup
Chopped chives and cream for garnish

Method
Melt the butter in a large pan.

Add the thinly sliced well washed leeks, and peeled and diced potato. Sweat covered with wetted greaseproof paper placed over the vegetables under the pan lid, over a low heat for about 8 minutes.

Add the stock, bay leaf and salt. Simmer for about 20 minutes.

Remove from the heat and discard the bay leaf.

Add milk and a little cornflour mixed in a little milk to thicken slightly.

Check seasoning and pass through an electric blender (reserving a few small pieces of leek and potato cubes to re-add to the blend).

Reheat and garnish with chopped chives and a swirl of cream.

This can be served chilled.

Good King Henry's Plait

In the autumn of 1402, Henry, Prince of Wales and afterwards King Henry V, stationed his army here to watch the movements of the Welsh general Owen Glyndwr. I like to imagine that Henry would have been entertained in the fourteenth century Great Hall, which is all that remains of the gabled building which then stood on the site.

In honour of our potential visitor I have created this rustic loaf of bread, which I choose to serve on a pewter platter with a fresh milky piece of caerphilly cheese, and perhaps a cox's pippin apple.

Ingredients

400g or 14 oz wholemeal flour
55g or 2 oz fine bran
225g or 8 oz granary flour
225g or 8 oz jumbo oats
1 level dsp salt
1 tbs caraway seeds
1 tsp ground caraway (optional)
575ml or 1 pt hand hot water,
    or half and half of water and semi-skimmed milk
25g or 1 oz fresh yeast
1 tbs honey
1 tbs oil or 25g or 1oz lard rubbed in
1 tbs milk and an egg for a glaze

Method

Mix yeast with a little of the hand hot water and leave 5 minutes.

Mix dry ingredients in a bowl. Add yeast, oil, milk, honey and water.

1 minute. Using the dough hook on an electric food mixer, mix until the dough leaves the sides of the bowl clean.

8 minutes. Place the dough onto a lightly floured table and follow the kneading method of turning, folding, pushing and crashing the dough on the table for at least 8 minutes. Place in a clean greased bowl. Pat with greased fingers to prevent crust, and cover with cling film.

First rising. One and half hours approx. (Do finger dent test at edges.) Place hot water tray in oven, warm oven to 400°F, 200°C, gas mark 6. (The American master baker Bernard Clayton recommends the use of a steam pan in electric ovens, as it otherwise tends to be such a dry heat.) Knead again (turn, fold, crash) for 10 minutes. Roll into three 24 inch strips, form into a ring, or cottage loaf or two plaits. Place on a greased tray. Cover with dry cloth or foil.

Second rising. Leave between 30 and 50 minutes until doubled in size. Glaze with the egg and 1 tbs of milk. Sprinkle with jumbo oats and caraway seeds (optional).

Bake at 400°F, 200°C, gas mark 6 for 30 to 40 minutes. Remove hot water pan after 20 minutes, and turn around if baking too quickly. Cool on a wire rack.

Wye Salmon Flan

'There is a river in Macedon: and there is also moreover a river at Monmouth, it is called Wye at Monmouth; but it is out of my brains what is the name of the other river; but 'tis all one; 'tis alike as my fingers to my fingers, and there is salmon in both!' *Henry V Act IV Scene V*

Ingredients (Serves 6)

225g or 8 oz rich shortcrust pastry
225g or half lb fresh Wye salmon
450ml or three-quarters pint milk
Blade of mace
6 white peppercorns
450 ml or three-quarters pint béchamel sauce
    (using the milk from poaching the salmon)

150ml or quarter pt mayonnaise
    (home-made if possible)
2 hard boiled eggs, finely chopped
1 tbs freshly chopped fennel

For the béchamel sauce
45g or 1 and a half oz flour
45g or 1 and a half oz butter
Milk from poaching the salmon

For the flan pastry
225g or 8 oz plain flour
115g or 4 oz butter
1 tbs icing sugar
2 egg yolks beaten with 2 tbs very cold water

Method

Line a 10 inch flan ring with the pastry, prick the base and cover with greaseproof paper and weigh down with baking beans. Bake at 190°C, 375°F, gas mark 5 for 30 to 40 minutes.

Poach the salmon in milk infused with the fennel stalks (reserving the leaves), white peppercorns and blade of mace for approximately 20 minutes.

Bone, flake and set aside the fish.

Make up the sauce (refer to page 85 if in doubt how to make) using the strained infused milk and add the mayonnaise. Season well.

Add the chopped fennel and the finely chopped eggs.

Place the flaked salmon in the pastry case and pour over the sauce. Serve warm with new potatoes and a tossed salad.

The most perfect salmon flan that I have ever tasted was created by the French born Madelaine Stratton of the famed Bell House Hotel at Sutton Benger, near Chippenham in Wiltshire. In 1962 it was my good fortune to obtain the Wine and Food Society's public relations account and I was invited to the hotel for a dinner organised by the Bath and Bristol branch. I found myself travelling down on the same train as the president of the society, André Simon, and an enthusiastic young wine writer, Hugh Johnson.

Knights of St. John Pie

Here I have created a pie which gives an excellent marriage of black treacle and rum. Suitable for yuletide!

Herefordshire is rich in the history of the ancient order of St. John which arose out of the Crusades to the Holy Land. The Knights Templar were the military order, the Knights Hospitaller of St. John were devoted to nursing and the care of the sick and the wounded.

At the beginning of the sixteenth century the order had reached its height of prosperity. The commandery at Dinmore Manor in Herefordshire was owned by Sir Thomas Docwra who survived the siege of Rhodes in 1480. He became a favourite of King Henry VIII and in 1501 became the Grand Prior of England, and generously rebuilt the priory headquarters at Clerkenwell in London from his own funds.

Ingredients for the pastry (Serves 6)
225g or 8 oz plain flour
3 tbs caster sugar
140g or 5 ozs grated frozen butter
Rind and some juice of an orange
1 egg, beaten

For the filling
2 tbs black treacle
3 size 3 eggs
1 to 2 tbs single cream
1 tbs rum (or a few drops of rum essence)
Rind and 1 tbs lemon juice
5 to 6 tbs soft breadcrumbs

For the topping
115 to 140g or 4 to 5 oz white marzipan
85g or 3 oz pecan nuts or flaked almonds

Method

Sift the flour, add the sugar, frozen grated butter and the rind of the orange. Make a well in the centre and gradually add the beaten egg, orange juice and a little water to form a firm dough.

Chill for at least half an hour.

Meanwhile roll out the marzipan. Using a template or peice of cardboard prepare the outline of one of the sections of the eight pointed star, cut from a 9 inch circle. Cut four sections to form the star, using any left over pieces of the marzipan for a centre rosette.

Line a greased 9 and a half inch loose bottomed flan tin with the chilled pastry.

Bake blind for 10 minutes in a hot oven, 425°F, 220°C, gas mark 6 to 7.

Combine the warmed treacle, beaten eggs, cream, rum essence or rum, lemon rind and juice over the half-cooked pastry. Cover with the breadcrumbs and place the prepared marzipan sections on top, filling the gaps with the pecan nuts or almonds. Place the rosette in the middle (see photograph).

Brush with a little left over beaten egg or milk.

Return to the centre of the oven for a further 10 to 15 minutes, or until the egg based filling feels cooked.

Leave to cool before removing from the flan ring, and dust with a little icing sugar.

Serve warm with whipped cream, egg-custard or a rum flavoured ground rice sauce.

Badger Sets and Squares

The good work and organisation of St. John still flourishes today. As president of the Hereford City Cadets, I have styled the following little cakes for the Badger group recently formed for the under sevens. Many of the cadets go on to take up nursing as a career.

Ingredients
170g or 6 oz self-raising flour
1 and a half tsp baking powder
3 large eggs
170g or 6 oz caster sugar
170g or 6 oz soft margarine
1 and a half tbs cocoa powder
4 tsp warm water

For the fudge icing and finish
225g or 8 oz white icing sugar
25g or 1 oz dark cooking chocolate
15g or half oz butter
125g or 4 and a half oz sifted icing sugar
1 tbs milk
A few chocolate chips and buttons

Method
Lightly grease a lamington or swiss roll tin which measures 16cm by 26cm.

Sift the flour and baking powder into a large bowl, add all the other ingredients to the bowl and whisk with an electric hand wisk until thoroughly combined, then add a few drops of warm water and whisk again.

Place in the tin and cook in the centre of the oven for about 30 minutes at 325°F, 170°C or gas mark 3.

When cooked, leave in the tin for 1 minute before turning out onto a wire tray to cool.

Ice the top with white icing, allowing to dry and cut into rectangles.

Melt the chocolate and butter over hot water, stir in the icing sugar and the milk. Apply the chocolate fudge strips and chocolate chips for eyes and buttons for ears and noses (see illustration overleaf).

A Mediaeval Salad Bowl

The following recipe has been compiled from a mediaeval salad given in John Russell's *Boke of Nurture* dated circa 1460.

Take some or all of the fresh vegetables and herbs listed below:

Parsley, sage, garlic, spring onions, leeks, baby onions, purslane, fennel, borage, mint, watercress, rue, rosemary, nasturtium leaves and a few of their flower heads, and a few lettuce leaves.

Wash and clean the vegetables and herbs. Prepare and slice the vegetables thinly, and grate the garlic. Shred the herbs by hand. Mix in enough olive or walnut oil to moisten. Sprinkle over a little white wine vinegar and salt, and serve immediately, or in fifteenth century terminology, 'Lay on vynegar and salt and serve it forth.'

The Elizabethan Era

During the Wars of the Roses and after, the manor passed to various owners including the Mortimers, the Devereux families, the Marchioness of Hertford and the Thynnes—the family of the Marquis of Bath, and the Earl of Essex.

The recipes in this section date from the time when, according to the manorial rolls, Burton Court was owned by Robert, third Earl of Essex, the son of Queen Elizabeth I's favourite. It is not known how much time the earl spent living at Burton Court, for he owned several residences.

In Thomas Dawson's *The Good Huswifes Jewell*, first printed in 1596 and republished in facsimile in 1977, there are various cures given in the section on husbandry. One, a sufferaine ointment for shrunken sinewes and aches, reads:

'Take eight swallowes ready to flye out of the nest, mine away the breeders when you take them out, and let them not touch the earth, stampe then untill the feathers cannot be perceived put to it lavender cotton, of ther stringes of strawberies, the tops of mother time, the toppes of Rosemarye, o eache a handfull, take all their weight of May butter, and a quarte more, stampe all the Fethers that nothing can be perceived, in a stone morter, then make it up in bales, and put it into an Earthen potte for eight days close topped that no ayre take them, take it out, and on as softe fire as my be seethe it, so that it does but simper, then strain it, and to reserve it to your use.'

More palatably the book also includes a Tarte of Strawberries:

'Take strawberries and washe them in claret wine, thicke and temper them with rose-water, and season them with cinamon, sugar, and ginger, and spread it on the Tarte, and enclose the sides with butter, and salt on sugar and biskettes, and serve them so.'

This recipe actually has a delicious flavour enhancing the taste of the strawberries, though the rose-water, cinnamon and ginger must be used sparingly. I have not tried making the ointment.

A Spinach Flan

The orginal recipe, which I have updated, again comes from Thomas Dawson's *The Good Huswifes Jewell* published in 1596. The original states 'To make a tarte of spinnage, when it is boyled, put away the water from it and put the spinnage in a stone morter, grind it smal with two dishes of butter melted, and four rawe eggs all to be beaten, then strain it and season it with sugar, Sinamon and ginger, and lay it in your coffin, when it is hardened in the oven, then bake it, and when it is enough serve it upon a faire dish, and cast upon it Suger and Biskets.'

Ingredients for the pastry (Serves 6)
150g or 6 oz plain flour
45g or 1 and a half oz lard
45g or 1 and a half oz butter or margarine
A pinch of salt
3 tbs cold water to mix

For the filling
170g or 6 oz fresh spinach
4 eggs, size 2
85g or 3 oz butter, melted
1 and a half tsp cinnamon
1 and a half tsp ground ginger
Caster sugar to finish (optional)

Method
Line an 8 inch flan ring with the pastry (see page 51 if need to know how), and bake blind for between 10 and 15 minutes at 220°C, 425°F or gas mark 7.

Wash the spinach and place in a saucepan with only the water that clings to the leaves. Slowly bring to the boil, stirring occasionally, and simmer for between 10 and 15 minutes until tender.

Drain the spinach and allow to cool before blending with the remaining ingredients to produce a smooth dark green mixture. I like to use an electric blender.

Spread the mixture evenly onto the prepared flan, and bake for between 30 and 40 minutes at 180°C, 350°F or gas mark 4.

If you wish, sprinkle a little caster sugar over the flan just before you serve it.

Celery and Coriander Soup

This is a very delicate tasting soup.

Ingredients (serves 4)
1 head of celery
850ml or 1 and a half pints white stock
25g or 1 oz flour
55g or 2 oz butter
150ml or quarter pint milk
1 tbs freshly chopped coriander
150ml or quarter pint single cream
Seasonings, a pinch of celery salt
Pinch of cayenne pepper for garnish

Method
Slice the celery into very thin pieces and simmer it in the stock until tender. You can then sieve it, but leave a few pieces for the final garnish.
Make a white sauce from the flour, butter and milk.
Slowly blend the celery purée mixture into the sauce.
Add the chopped coriander and reheat, then add the cream and seasonings.
Garnish with a few pieces of chopped celery and a sprinkling of cayenne pepper.

Parsnip and Hazelnut Fritters

Before the arrival of the potato in this country, carrots and parsnips were used in a variety of ways to sweeten and accompany many meat dishes. These are good served with roast pheasant.

Ingredients (makes 12 rolls)
1kg or 2 to 2 and half pounds parsnips
2 eggs
1 tbs flour
85g or 3 oz butter
450ml or three-quarters pint milk
Grated nutmeg
Seasonings
115g or 4 oz roasted hazelnuts

Method
Purée the cooked parsnips, then mix in all the other ingredients well.
Form into twelve rolls, flour well and deep fry. Drain on kitchen paper.
These can be frozen and then warmed up.

Chicken in a Gooseberry and Elderflower sauce

This is derived from a book of recipes written by Lady Elinor Fettiplace in 1604. She came from Pauntley in Gloucestershire, just over the boundary with Herefordshire, and was the granddaughter of Sir Richard Whittington, better known as Dick Whittington, who set out from Pauntley for London where he became mayor three times in the fourteenth century.

As with many early cookery manuscripts there is a list of cures. Her uncle by marriage, Sir Walter Raleigh, provided her with Tobacco Syrup, a cure for lung trouble, and tobacco water, a potent alcoholic cordial. The attribution to Raleigh is in Lady Fettiplace's own writing, the majority of the manuscript in that of her scribe. She also gives a recipe for Spanish marmalade, listing amongst the ingredients powdered seed pearls and three sheets of gold leaf. Expensive marmalade!

There is an affinity between gooseberries and elderflowers, and if a muscatel wine is added, as I suggest, this can enhance the flavour and fragrance of the elderflowers.

Ingredients (Serves 4)
4 chicken joints
55g or 2 oz butter
1 medium onion, finely chopped
300ml or half a pint Muscatel or sweet wine
2 bay leaves
1 tbs lemon juice
Watercress for garnish

For the purée
6 elderflower heads
225g or 8 oz gooseberries
150ml or quarter pint water
55g or 2 oz granulated sugar
150ml or quarter pint double cream

Method
Prepare the purée. Dissolve the sugar in the water, drop in the top and tailed gooseberries and the elderflowers without their stalks. (Keep the stalks for use later). Lower the heat and cook for 10 minutes. Let it cool and then pass through the blender and sieve.

Gently fry the chopped onion in the butter until golden brown, but do not burn.

Season the chicken joints with salt and pepper and fry them over a low heat with the butter and onions for about 25 minutes until cooked thoroughly, turning occasionally.

Transfer the contents of the pan to a large pot and add the wine, bay leaves and elderflower stalks. Simmer, covered, over a low heat for 15 minutes.

Remove the chicken joints and place on a warmed serving dish. Discard the bay leaves and elderflower stalks and add the gooseberry and elderflower purée to the pot juices. Add the cream, season to taste, then add the lemon juice and reheat.

Pour the sauce over the chicken joints, garnish with watercress and serve.

An Egg Nog Pudding with Orange Finger Biscuits

Egg nogs or egg punches have been part of English cooking for centuries, often being used to aid patients' recovery. In her 1604 book, Lady Fettiplace gives the following egg nog cure for a 'great' cold. 'Take the yolk of an egg, and one spoonfull of aqua vitae, and foure spoonfulls of goats or cowe milk, hot from the cowe, beat it all together, and then drink it fasting and last at night.'

By the twentieth century it had become a pudding, whilst in Italy they were adding Marsala wine and calling it Zabaglione. I was shown the Italian way in the early 1950's by the well-known chef Calderoni of London's Mayfair Hotel. I was working as a secretary, often typing the next day's menu proofs which resulted in daily journeys through the kitchens to his office.

At the time Calderoni was joining forces with Jean Nicol, the Maître des Cuisines at Fortnum & Mason to found the International Academy of Chefs de Cuisine in London. Changes were taking place with deep freezes leading to a wider choice of ingredients, and it is through these two men that the Salon Culinaire International de Londres is held at Hotelympia every two years, where there are endless spun sugar and epicurean delights.

All true cooks appreciate there are certain dishes that have to be stood over with patience to prevent curdling, for example Sauce Hollandaise, and of course this pudding. The old adage 'Guests must be seated waiting for the dish, not the dish waiting for the guests' applies here. It is best to allow two egg yolks per person and serve it hot. The recipe for orange finger biscuits which follows goes well with this pudding.

Ingredients (for each person)
2 egg yolks
2 tbs caster sugar
2 tbs of good sherry or madeira
    (Brandy, rum, whisky or Marsala wine can be used)

Method
Beat together the egg yolks and sugar until they are pale and creamy.

Slowly stir in the wine and place the whole mixture over hot water in a double boiler. Like a custard stir continuously until it thickens, taking care that it does not boil and curdle.

Serve immediately in tall warmed glasses with sponge fingers, crispin biscuits or orange finger biscuits.

Orange Finger Biscuits

Ingredients (Makes about 40)
225g or 8 oz self-raising flour
140g or 5 oz margarine
140g or 5 oz caster sugar
Grated rind of 2 oranges
1 standard egg
1 tbs orange juice

Method
Prepare a moderate oven, 375°F, 180°C, or gas mark 5 and grease two baking sheets.

Place the flour in a bowl, add the margarine, cut into small pieces, and rub in with fingertips until the mixture resembles fine breadcrumbs. Mix in the sugar and orange rinds.

Separate the egg and place the white in a small basin and beat lightly with a fork. Beat the egg yolk and orange juice together, add to the dry ingredients in the bowl and mix to a firm dough.

Turn out onto a floured board and knead until smooth. Roll out to an eighth of an inch thickness, brush with the egg white and sprinkle with caster sugar.

Cut into rounds with a 2 inch fluted cutter or into fingers. Knead together trimmings and roll out again. Repeat brushing with egg white and sprinkling with sugar. Place a little apart on baking sheets.

Bake for 12 to 15 minutes until pale golden brown. Cool on wire racks and store in air-tight containers.

Herefordshire Trout in Cider, with Almond Sauce

Ingredients (serves 4)

4 medium trout
300ml or half a pint fish stock
300ml or half a pint dry cider
Fennel stalk
1 bay leaf
450ml or three-quarters of a pint
  béchamel sauce made from the stock
85g or 3 oz toasted flaked almonds
Squeeze of lemon juice
Dash of almond essence
Seasoning
150ml or quarter pint double cream

For the stuffing for each trout
2 cloves
Sprig of thyme
Pinch of cinnamon

Method

Into the cleaned trout place the cloves, sprig of thyme and a pinch of cinnamon.

Poach the trout in the stock, cider, bay leaf and fennel for 30 minutes so that it is just simmering.

Strain onto a warmed dish and make up the sauce from the poaching juices (see page 85 if in doubt as to how) adding two-thirds of the toasted almonds, the essence and lemon juice, and lastly add the cream.

Heat and pour over the fish and garnish with the remaining almonds and some chopped parsley.

Apple and Blackberry (or Damson) Tansy

I have served this Elizabethan styled pudding many times to overseas guests. With a rosette of whipped cream piped on top, the colour is magnificent. The recipe gets its name from the bitter-tasting herb the tansy, widely used in flavouring sweets where sometimes spinach was also added. However, it is now descriptive of buttered fruit purées using eggs and breadcrumbs.

This recipe works just as well with loganberries, tayberries, raspberries, damsons or plums.

Ingredients (Serves 4 to 6)
225g or 8 oz blackberries or damsons
225g or 8 oz cooking apples
55g or 2 oz unsalted butter
115g or 4 oz caster sugar
2 egg yolks
4 level dsps fresh white or brown breadcrumbs
150ml or quarter pt double cream
1 dsp lemon juice

Method
Wash the fruit, reserving a few for a final garnish.

Peel, core and thinly slice the apples.

Melt the butter in a saucepan with 3 and a half tablespoons of cold water. Add the fruit, then cover and boil over a low heat until soft, stirring occasionally.

Remove the pan from the heat and rub the fruit through a coarse sieve.

Return the purée to the pan and stir in the sugar to taste. If the purée is thin, cook it over a low heat until it has reduced.

Take the pan off the heat and blend in the beaten egg yolks and the breadcrumbs.

Stir the mixture over a low heat until quite thick, then leave to cool.

Whisk the cream lightly and fold it into the cooked purée. Sharpen the taste with lemon juice.

Spoon the mixture into the serving glasses and chill in the refrigerator for at least one hour.

Before serving, pipe whipped cream on top and decorate with a few of the reserved blackberries.

Flan of Marigold or Cowslip flowers

I know a bank whereon the wild thyme blows,
Where ox-lips and the nodding violet grows
A Midsummer Night's Dream Act II, Scene II

This recipe originates in a sixteenth century book the *Proper Newe Booke of Cokerye* held in the library of Corpus Christi College, Cambridge and called for the uncooked egg yolks to be added to the cooking apples and mace. I have adapted it to include a Crème Anglaise sauce, deleting the vanilla, so that the eggs are cooked.

If you are concerned at the use of fresh cowslip flowers from the countryside, dried marigold petals can be obtained from Culpeppers, whose address is given at the end of the book.

Ingredients for the pastry (Serves 6 to 8)
(for a 9 and a half inch flan tin)
225g or 8 oz self-raising flour
85g or 3 oz icing sugar
1 level tsp cinnamon
85g or 3 oz jumbo oats
225g or 8 oz unsalted butter, semi-frozen
2 egg yolks, beaten with 2 tsp water

For the Crème Anglaise
300ml or half pint milk
3 egg yolks
25g or 1 oz flour
115g or 4 oz caster sugar

For the filling
1 handful of marigold, cowslip or borage flowers
3 to 4 medium cooking apples
A walnut of unsalted butter
A generous pinch of powdered mace

Method for the pastry

Sift the flour, icing sugar and cinnamon together, then add the oats.

Grate in the semi-frozen butter, and mix round lightly with the fingers till the butter is well distributed.

Add the egg yolks and water and lightly form into a ball.

Chill overnight or for at least six hours.

Roll out at room temperature and line the greased flan dish. Chill again for half an hour.

Line the pastry with foil and weigh down with baking beans and bake blind for 30 to 35 minutes at 325°F, 160°C or gas mark 3, then leave to cool.

Method for the Crème Anglaise

Whisk the eggs, flour and sugar.

Slowly heat the milk, and allow to come to just below boiling.

Pour the heated milk onto the egg mixture and stir thoroughly.

Turn into the top of a double saucepan over hot water and stir until the mixture becomes thick and creamy and coats the back of a wooden stirring spoon.

Allow to cool, covering the surface with cling film to stop a skin forming.

Method for filling

Peel and slice the apples thinly, and poach until tender in very little water. Simmer the flower heads in water until tender.

Strain them and add to the cooked apple, mix in the butter and mace and add to the cooling Crème Anglaise.

Fill the prepared pastry case and decorate with crystalised flower heads and a sprig of mint.

Serve with whipped cream.

Shrewsbury Tarts

The pastry calls for a dough that is crisp but not flaky, so a paté brisée is best.

Ingredients for the pastry (makes 12 tartlets)
225g 8 oz plain flour
Half tsp salt
1 tbs granulated sugar
115g or 4 oz unsalted butter chilled
25g or 1 oz lard or margarine
1 egg lightly beaten
1 tsp lemon juice
2 tbs iced water

For the filling
225g or 8 oz cream cheese
55g or 2 oz granulated sugar
55g or 2 oz butter
Quarter tsp salt
Pinch of nutmeg
2 egg yolks
1 tbs orange juice
Half tsp grated orange rind
6 oz or 170 g apricot jam
1 tbs brandy

Method
Work the butter and lard into the sifted flour, salt and sugar, a pastry blender is excellent, until the mixture resembles breadcrumbs.

Combine the beaten egg, lemon juice and 1 tbs iced water and slowly pour the mixture into the flour and fat mixture with a fork. The mixture should then hold together in a rough mass. If too crumbly dry, add a little more water. It will stiffen when chilled.

Using 3 inch tartlet tins, line the tins with the rolled out pastry, shaping to fit the forms.

Partially bake the unfilled tartlet shells at 425°F, 220°C or gas mark 7, filling them with protective foil or kitchen paper and baking beans. Place in the oven for 10 minutes.

Reduce heat to 375°F, 190°C or gas mark 5.

Remove baking beans and set aside.

In a food processor cream together the filling ingredients—the cream cheese, sugar, butter, salt, nutmeg, egg yolks, orange juice and grated orange rind.

Place approximately 1 tbs filling in each tartlet and cook for a further 15 minutes.

Meanwhile make an apricot glaze. Press the apricot jam through a sieve and into a small saucepan. Bring the jam to the boil over a medium heat and stir in the brandy. When still hot, brush the hot pastries with the glaze.

The Making of a Pomander

In the sixteenth century a perfumed ball, or small box or bag containing perfumed powder, was sometimes carried around the neck to ward off infection and unpleasant smells. By courtesy of *Woman and Home* magazine here is a recipe for a pomander that will give your kitchen a wonderful fragrance, or keep the moths out of your wardrobe.

Ingredients
1 firm thin skinned orange
25g or 1 oz whole cloves
55g or 2 oz cinnamon
55g or 2 oz orris root
(available from Culpeppers)

Method
For one that will be hung, first tie two ribbons at right angles to each other around the fruit, or use two pieces of sellotape. Marking the quarters, insert the cloves as below working around the straight lines of the ribbons or tape.

Pierce the skin of the orange in neat rows with a knitting needle and insert cloves into the holes, leaving a little space between each clove as the orange will shrink slightly as it dries out.

Continue until the quarters, or in the case of one to be used in a box or jar the whole orange is completely covered.

Mix together the cinnamon and orris root powders in a bowl and roll the clove-studded orange in the powder until well coated.

Wrap in tissue-paper and place in a warm, dark place, for six to eight weeks. An airing cupboard is ideal.

Unwrap and shake off the excess powder, which can be used again if stored in an airtight jar.

For the hanging variety—tie with fresh ribbons and a long tie so that it can be hung up easily.

Maid-of-Honour Tarts

During the reign of Henry VIII these tarts were very popular with the queens' maids-of-honour at Hampton Court Palace, hence their name. It is also thought that Elizabeth I liked them as her ladies-in-waiting were sent to collect them from a certain baker in Richmond town. Maybe Robert, third Earl of Essex, the son of Queen Elizabeth's favourite, enjoyed eating them at Burton Court. Today's recipes vary, but here is the traditional one which should be made with ground almonds, curd cheese and flavoured with brandy.

Ingredients (Makes 16)
225g or 8 oz frozen or home-made puff pastry
115g or 4 oz curd cheese
75g or 3 oz butter, softened
2 egg yolks
1 tbs brandy
85g or 3 oz caster sugar
45g or 1 and a half oz cold mashed potato
45g or 1 and a half oz ground almonds
Grated rind of half a lemon
1 tbs lemon juice
Pinch of freshly grated nutmeg
1 tsp rosewater

Method
Roll out the pastry and line 16 patty tins.

Beat the cheese and butter together until smooth, then gradually beat in the egg yolks and brandy.

Add the sugar, potato, almonds, lemon rind, juice, nutmeg and rosewater and beat until smooth.

Spoon the mixture into the pastry cases and bake in a moderate oven, 190°C, 375°F, gas mark 5, for about 30 minutes, until well risen and golden brown.

Cool on a wire rack. They will sink back slightly whilst cooling, but this is correct.

Carp Leon Valley

'Your bait of falsehood takes the carp of truth' *Hamlet Act II, Scene I*

In 1653 Izaak Walton's *The Compleat Angler* was published. A recipe for carp appears requiring the fish to be stuffed with sweet marjoram, thyme, parsley, rosemary, savory, onions, oysters, eggs, anchovies and cooked in claret. Even more elaborate was a recipe for pike which was adjudged 'a dish of meat too good for any but anglers or very honest men.'

Between 1850 and 1920 the Poncelet water wheel, still in place today, pumped water to the Court from our lake. Now the lake is given over to coarse fishing and stocked with carp, for which this recipe follows, though coley, monkfish or fillets of trout could be an alternative. An apple juice of coxs and bramleys, as made at the nearby Dinmore Fruit Farm, makes a delicious sauce.

Ingredients (Serves 4)
1.7 to 2.3kg or 4 to 5 lb carp,
    or 450g or 1 lb white fish fillets per person
Seasoned flour
1 dsp vinegar
300ml or half pint milk
150ml or quarter pint cox and bramley apple juice
1 bay leaf
30g or 1oz cornflour
1 level tbs capers
4 tsp chopped parsley
1 small tin anchovies
Freshly ground pepper
55g or 2 oz breadcrumbs
30g or 1 oz grated parmesan cheese

Method
After scaling and cleaning the carp, soak it using two lots of salted water, and lastly in a dessertspoon of vinegar and salted water.

Cut the fish fillets into 3 inch strips and roll them in seasoned flour (for the recipe for this see page 45), and place in a baking dish covered with the milk, apple juice and bay leaf. Poach gently for 10 minutes.

Remove the bay leaf and pour off the liquid to make a sauce. Keep the fish warm. Add the cornflour blended with 1 tablespoon of water to the sauce and stirring cook for 5 minutes. Add the capers, chopped parsley and the chopped anchovies and their oil. Add some freshly ground pepper to taste and place the sauce over the fish.

Sprinkle the mixture of breadcrumbs and parmesan cheese over the top, and dot with some butter.

Return to the oven at 180°C, 350°F, gas mark 4, for 20 minutes until golden brown.

Serve with shredded cooked cabbage and sauté potatoes.

Cider poached Bream with fruit

The sauce for this dish is based on a recipe by Gervase Markham in his *A Way to Health*, published in 1660. Instead of verjuice which was made with crab apples, I have used Herefordshire cider, but you may use a pint of water and two tablespoons of cider vinegar. The sauce is colourful, and good with fillets of trout as well.

Ingredients (Serves 4)
450g or 1lb filleted bream or trout
575ml or 1 pint dry Herefordshire cider
1 tsp salt
115g or 4 oz finely sliced onion
55g or 2 oz currants soaked overnight in some cider
30g or 1 oz redcurrants
1 tbs cornflour
1 tbs water
55g or 2 oz chopped fresh dates
55g or 2 oz cooked and stoned chopped prunes

Method
Poach the bream in the cider with the salt and onion. Remove the fish and keep hot.

Add the soaked currants and the redcurrants to the pan and simmer for 5 minutes. Mix the cornflour and water to a paste and add to the sauce, stirring to thicken.

Arrange the chopped prunes and dates on top of the fish fillets and pour the sauce over. Reheat and serve garnished with watercress.

Menu for an Elizabethan Banquet held in the Great Hall at Burton Court in April 1982

(in aid of the St. John Ambulance Association)

Beef and Barley Broth

***

Galantine of Eel
Chicken Drumsticks
Game Pie

Parsnip & Hazlenut Fritters
Red Cabbage Compote
Spinach Flan

***

Fruit Tansy
Shrewsbury & Maid-of-Honour Tarts

***

Elizabethan Sweetmeats

***

Mulled Wine

Come now; what masks, what dances shall we have
To wear away this long age of three hours
Between our after-supper and bed-time?

The Seventeenth & Eighteenth Centuries

Only two families were squires of Eardisland and lords of the manor of Burton from 1660 to 1950, the Brewsters until 1885 and then the Clowes family.

Dr. William Brewster was born at the Court in 1665. He became an eminent scholar as well as one of Hereford's practising doctors and the city's mayor. He donated the famous chained library to All Saints Church in Hereford, and when he died in 1715 he left many of his books to the Bodleian Library and to St. John's College, also in Oxford.

Eventually the last Brewster heiress married the Rev. Canon W.E. Evans, described as the talented pious author of *The Song of the Birds*, and a close observer of nature. They were not survived by any children.

This Brewster period was a time when advances were made in the preservation of food. The present Lord Croft's sister, the Hon. Diana Uhlman, told me that around the 1750's packmen arrived at Croft Castle carrying pickled salmon in barrels. These were sent in large quantities to the then owner, Thomas Johnes the elder, as a gift from his brother, John Johnes, who owned the estate of Dolecothy in Carmarthenshire, an estate which included a gold mine. In return the packmen would carry collars of brawn back to Wales. One gathers from letters sent to his brother that Thomas Johnes also arranged for pickled salmon to be delivered to influential members of parliament, doubtless with an eye to advancing his own and his son's political ambitions.

There was also no shortage of cookery books, one of the most popular being Hannah Glasse's manual *The Art of Cookery made Plain and Easy*. It was first published in 1747 and was republished several times thereafter during the following hundred years. Hannah Glasse complains bitterly about the extravagance of French recipes, then influencing English cookery. There were three main culprits. The first, La Varenne, famed for his pastry shells, had published *The French Cook* many years before and which by 1653 had also been published in English. The other two, Anton Carême and George Auguste Escoffier were to make an even greater impact over the years.

In England William Verrall published his recipes in his *Cookery Book* of 1759. He had also come under French influence for he had been an apprentice to the French cook St. Clouet in the Duke of Newcastle's kitchens before becoming the innkeeper of the White Hart Inn in Lewes, Sussex.

At the time of the French Revolution many French chefs fled to England and found employment with the English nobility. Homesick and often feeling their skills went unappreciated in England, many returned after the Revolution. But their influence remained.

At the White Hart Inn Verrall was serving Gros Entrées, Petrits Entrées and Hors d'oeuvres. Tastes have since changed, or perhaps the best food has become proportionately cheaper, for many of his recipes would be unacceptable today. For example lambs ears with sorrel, or turtle, even a dish of calves tails with carrots in a brown sauce.

Others are much more presentable, especially if you scale down the quantities. All his fruit fritter recipes are highly acceptable!

William Verrall's Strawberry Fritters

'For this you must make a batter of another sort from what you have seen before; to two eggs well beat, white and yolks both, put about half a pint of cream, made thick with fine flour, a little fine sugar and nutmeg, put your strawberries in raw, and fry them in a pan of clean lard, a spoonful at a time, dish them up in a pyramid, and sift sugar between and at top.' This is my updated version, using beer in the batter which gives a lighter touch.

Ingredients (Serves 4)
450g or 1lb strawberries (of roughly equal size)
Juice of a lemon
Icing-sugar
115g or 4 oz sifted flour
Half a level tsp salt
1 tbs olive oil
1 egg
Enough beer to make a good coating consistency

Method
Sift the flour and salt into a bowl. Gradually add the beaten egg, olive oil and enough beer to make a good coating consistency. Leave to stand for at least two hours.

Steep the strawberries in the lemon juice for half an hour.

Roll them in some sifted icing-sugar and pass through the batter a few at a time and deep fry in hot oil, or shallow fry for about 5 minutes until really crispy. Drain and place on a kitchen towel and keep warm.

For serving pile up in a pyramid shape on a raised dish and coat liberally with sifted icing sugar.

Serve with lightly whipped cream flavoured with kirsch or brandy.

Chilled Orange & Ginger Cream

In 1660 Charles II pioneered the first ice-house in Britain, which he included in his improvements to St. James's Park. The first ice-cream is recorded to have been eaten at Windsor Castle seven years later.

The great country houses of the land soon built their own ice-houses, marking a turning point in the history of culinary skills. Not only could food be kept fresh for longer periods, but people began to enjoy iced puddings, drinks and creams in the heat of summer.

Ingredients (Serves 2 to 4)
2 eggs
2 tbs caster sugar
150ml or quarter pt milk
11g or 0.4 oz gelatine
2 tbs water
1 tbs orange juice
150ml or quarter pint whipped cream
2 tbs orange curacao
55g or 2 oz preserved ginger, chopped
Rind of an orange
Half tsp ground ginger

Method
Separate the eggs and stir the sugar into the yolks. Blend thoroughly.

Bring milk just to the boil and pour steadily into the yolk mixture, stirring all the time.

Heat in a double boiler stirring until thickened enough to thinly coat the back of a wooden spoon, but do not allow to boil or it will curdle.

Remove from the heat and stir in the gelatine dissolved in the water and orange juice.

Strain and stand in a cool place until just on the point of setting.

Fold in the whipped cream, stiffly beaten egg whites, orange curacao, chopped ginger, ground ginger and the orange rind.

Turn into a prepared mould and chill in the refrigerator until the cream has set.

Caraway Cheese Stars & Moons

Ground caraway or its seeds were often in use and flavoured many dishes. These cheese pastries are very rich in protein.

Ingredients
115g or 4 oz plain flour
Seasonings
Pinch of cayenne pepper
Pinch of celery salt
55g or 2 oz butter
55g or 2 oz grated cheese
1 tbs water
1 egg yolk
Half tbs ground caraway or seeds
A few sesame seeds

Method
Sift flour and seasonings, then rub in the butter.
Add the grated cheese and mix the pastry with the water.
Roll out to a quarter inch thickness and cut with star and moon cutter shapes.
Glaze with milk and egg yolk, add a few sesame seeds, and bake in a hot oven 425°F, 220°C or gas mark 7 for 15 minutes. Cool on a wire rack.

Hereford Cider Syllabub

'Syllabub' is derived from an Elizabethan word for bubbling drinks. John Farley's *The London Art of Cookery*, 1783, gives one recipe named Syllabub under the Cow in which he asks 'Then milk the cow as much milk as will make a strong froth.' Do so if you wish!

Ingredients (Serves 6 to 8)
575ml or 1 pint thick double cream
300ml or half a pint sweet Herefordshire cider
Juice and rind of 1 lemon
1 tbs King Offa Cider Brandy
A little grated nutmeg

Method
Whip the cream in a chilled large mixing bowl.
Fold in the other ingredients and pour into individual glasses. Sprinkle a little freshly grated nutmeg over each glass and chill well before serving.

Elderflower Sorbet

Ingredients
About 6 heads of fresh elderflowers
170g or 6 oz honey or caster sugar
575ml or 1 pt water
Juice and grated rinds of 3 lemons
1 orange
1 egg white

Method
Place the elderflowers and honey or sugar in a saucepan with one pint of water. Bring to the boil and simmer for about 10 minutes.

Strain, add the lemon and orange juice and rinds. Freeze overnight.

Return from the freezer, beat in the stiffly whisked egg white and return to the freezer.

This can be served in sweetened filo pastry baskets or Prue Leith's filigree baskets (for this method refer to her book *Leith's Cookery School*).

Gooseberry and Ginger Ice Cream

This recipe of mine is very popular in our tea-room. The amount of ginger can be adjusted according to taste.

Ingredients
450g or 1 lb gooseberries
75ml or 3 fl oz water
1 tbs freshly grated root ginger
2 tsp powdered ginger
2 pieces of stem ginger (sliced very fine)
1 tbs stem ginger syrup
300ml or half a pint thick double cream
115g or 4 oz caster sugar
Juice of a lemon

Method
Stew the gooseberries in the water until the skins are tender.

Liquidize and pass through a sieve.

Pour the purée and the remaining ingredients into the ice-cream maker and churn for approximately 20 minutes.

Freeze.

Tayberry Whip

This recipe works very well with most soft fruit. I like to use tayberries for an interesting new flavour, but black and redcurrants are also ideal.

Ingredients (Serves 6)
450g or 1 lb tayberries
115g or 4 oz caster sugar
2 large eggs and 1 egg yolk
   (keep the white for decoration)
15g or half oz powdered gelatine
3 tbs water
100ml or 4 fl oz double cream
A few tayberries left on a stalk for decoration

Method

Wash the fruit, drain, put in a pan with the sugar and cook them over a low heat until soft and pulpy.

Liquidize and put through a sieve. Add the eggs and extra yolk and whisk over a pan of hot water until creamy and thick and doubled in bulk.

Melt the gelatine in the water in a small pan over a very low heat. Do not boil. Stir the gelatine into the purée and leave to cool until nearly set.

Pour the cream into a small bowl and whip until it just holds its shape, then using a metal spoon fold it into the almost set mousse.

Divide into sundae glasses and leave to set completely.

Just before serving, break up the egg white with a fork and beat in a teaspoon of water. Using a brush, paint the tayberries on stalks with the egg white and sprinkle them with caster sugar. Arrange some on each glass.

Potted Cheshire Cheese

In the seventeenth and eighteenth centuries potted meats and fish were popular. It proved a good way to preserve food for several weeks. In my facsimilie copy of Eliza Smith's *The Compleat Housewife* published in 1727, there is even a recipe called To Pot a Swan! In her best selling cookery book *The Art of Cookery made Plain and Easy*, Hannah Glasse gives several versions, but for a change try adding some halved hazlenuts, chopped walnuts or pecan nuts.

Ingredients
225g or 8 oz mature cheshire cheese
50 to 75g or 2 to 3 oz unsalted butter
30ml or 2 tbs sweet sherry
7ml or 1 rounded tsp ground mace
Clarified butter

Method
Grate the cheese finely and mix with the butter, which should be soft but not melted.
Add the sherry and mace and the nuts if used, and mix well.
Press down in a pot and cover with clarified butter.

Curried Parsnip and Carrot Soup

A delicious warming winter soup. In earlier centuries marigolds were closely associated with strength and courage and were dried to later use to flavour and add a saffron-colour to winter dishes, especially lentil soup and stews.

Ingredients (Serves 4)
1 large parsnip
1 large carrot
1 onion
85g or 3 oz butter
1 tbs plain flour
1 tsp hot curry powder
575ml or 1 pint stock
1 tbs marigold petals (available from Culpeppers)

Method
Slice the parsnip, carrot and onion and fry in the butter.
Add the flour, curry powder and stock, and simmer until the vegetables are soft.
Liquidize, add the marigold petals and reheat but don't let it boil.
Serve with croutons, and garnish with chopped chives.

Three of John Farley's recipes

John Farley, a celebrated cook at the City of London Tavern, published the popular *London Art of Cookery* in 1783. The tavern had been opened in 1768 and became famous for its wines, food and as a venue for public meetings. The Pillar Room could seat 300 'banqueters' along with 150 ladies as spectators in galleries at each end. Two tons of live turtles were said to have been kept at the ready in the wine cellar at 'an equal temperature of fifty-five degrees.' John Farley reigned over the kitchen and his book boasts that for the first time recipes are logically laid out and easy to follow.

A Solomon-Gundy

Take a handful of parsley, two pickled herrings, four boiled eggs, both yolks and whites, and the white part of a roasted chicken. Chop them separately, and exceedingly small. Take the lean of some boiled ham scraped fine, and turn a china bason upside down in the middle of the dish. Make a quarter of a pound of butter into the shape of a pineapple, and set it on the bason's bottom. Lay round your bason a ring of shred parsley, then a ring of yolks of eggs, then whites, then ham, then chickens, and then herrings till you have covered your bason, and disposed of all the ingredients. Lay the bones of the pickled herrings upon it, with their tails up to the butter, and let their heads lie on the edge of the dish. Lay a few capers and three or four pickled oysters round the dish.

A Dish of Snow

Put twelve large apples into cold water, set them over a slow fire, and when they be soft pour them upon a hair sieve. Take off the skins, and put the pulp into a bason. Then beat the whites of twelve eggs to a very strong froth, beat and sift a pound of double-refined sugar, and strew it onto the eggs. Then beat the pulp of your apples to a strong froth, then beat them all together till they be like a stiff snow, lay it upon a china dish, and heap it up as high as you can. Set round it green knots of paste in imitation Chinese rails, and stick a sprig of myrtle in the middle of the dish.

Duke of Cumberland's Pudding

Take flour, grated apples, currants, chopped suet, and sugar, of each six ounces; six eggs, a little nutmeg and salt. Boil it two hours at least, and serve it with melted butter, wine and sugar.

Tenderloin of Pork in Herefordshire Cider

Herefordshire is famed for its production of many types of cider, and it goes well with pork dishes. Not far from here the Dunkertons, a husband and wife team, have been replanting old species of cider apples from which they produce varietal ciders.

Ingredients (Serves 4)
450g or 1 lb tenderloin of pork
25g or 1 oz butter
1 tbs oil
1 medium onion
1 clove of garlic
300ml or half pint meat stock
300ml or half pint dry cider
Half tsp dried marjoram,
    or 1 dsp freshly chopped marjoram
170g or 6 oz button mushrooms
100ml or 4 fl oz double cream
1 tbs cornflour
4 pre-cooked king sized vol-au-vent cases
A little chopped parsley

For the seasoned flour
(This recipe of Fanny Craddock's makes about 3lbs; surplus can be kept in airtight jars)
900g or 2 lbs plain flour
140g or 5 oz sea salt
45g or 1 and a half oz coarsely ground black pepper
45g or 1 and a half oz dry English mustard
20g or three-quarters oz rose paprika
1 tsp dried basil, chervil, thyme and parsley

Method
Sift the flour with mustard, salt and pepper. Work in the rest of the ingredients and set the seasoned flour aside.

Melt the butter and oil and gently fry the finely sliced onion and garlic. Remove with a slotted spoon and set aside.

Remove all the surplus fat from the pork and cube into roughly inch and half sized pieces. Toss in seasoned flour and gently brown on all sides and place in a casserole dish with the onion, garlic and marjoram.

Pour over the stock and cider. Season well, and bake in a moderate oven, 350°F, 180°C or gas mark 4 for 20 minutes.

Add the sliced mushrooms, cornflour mixed with the cream to thicken and return to the oven for a further 15 minutes.

Serve in king sized vol-au-vent cases or filo pastry baskets. Garnish with chopped parsley.

Herefordshire Beef Chops

'The befe of Englande bringeth stronge nourishmente to those that are in helthe.'
  Sir Thomas Elyot, *A Castel of Helthe* 1538

This recipe is based on John Farley's recipe of 1783, and to his sauce I have added some chopped tomatoes. Tomatoes arrived in this country in the nineteenth century from South America via North Carolina. Known as love apples they were at first viewed with suspicion and were used more as a decoration, for were they a fruit or a vegetable?

Ingredients (Serves 4)
4 rump steaks
40g or 1 and a half oz flour
60g or 2 and a half oz softened butter
570ml or 1 pint good beef stock
4 gherkins, thinly sliced
2 to 3 skinned and chopped tomatoes
60g or 2 and a half oz onion, very finely chopped
Half a pickled walnut, crushed
1 tbs capers
Salt & pepper
Chopped parsley for a garnish

Method
Flatten the steaks well and score them with a knife.

Dust the steaks with some of the flour and fry them in 25g or 1 oz of butter in a very hot frying pan for 1 minute on each side, or longer if you want them well-done. Remove and keep them in a warm low oven.

Mix the remaining butter with the rest of the flour and add to the pan juices. Then add the beef stock, gherkins, tomatoes, onion, walnut and capers. Season well and cook for 5 minutes, and pour the sauce over the prepared steaks.

Garnish with a little fried chopped parsley and serve with duchess potatoes.

Ginger and Cinnamon Jumbles

Ginger and cinnamon have been used in English cookery for centuries and would have been in constant use by the seventeenth century. This recipe of mine makes about 40 biscuits which should be stored, if not eaten directly, in an airtight tin.

Ingredients (Makes 40 biscuits)
225g or 8 oz self-raising flour
140g or 5 oz margarine or butter
140g or 5 oz caster sugar
1 standard egg
1 tbs milk
115g or 4 oz chopped nuts
4 level tsp ground ginger
A few drops of ginger essence
Half tsp cinnamon
Pinch of salt

Method
Prepare a moderate oven, 375°F, 180°C or gas mark 5. Grease two baking sheets.

Place flour and seasonings in a bowl. Add margarine or butter cut in small pieces and rub in with your fingertips until the mixture resembles fine breadcrumbs. Mix in the chopped nuts, reserving some for a garnish, and the sugar.

Separate the egg, placing the white in a small basin and beat lightly with a fork. Beat the yolk and milk together and add to the dry ingredients and mix to form a dough.

Turn onto a floured board and knead until smooth. Roll out to an eighth of an inch thickness, brush with egg white and sprinkle with caster sugar.

Cut into rounds with a 2 inch fluted cutter. Knead together trimmings and roll out again and repeat. Brush with egg white and a sprinkling of sugar, then add the remaining chopped nuts. Place a little apart on baking sheets.

Bake from 12 to 15 minutes until pale golden brown. Cool on wire racks.

A King's Christmas Pudding

This special recipe dates from the reign of King George I when it was used in the royal kitchens, and has been in the possession of the royal family ever since.

Ingredients (Makes 3 puddings)

675g or 1 and a half lbs suet finely shredded
450g or 1 lb small raisins
450g or 1 lb demerara sugar
450g or 1 lb plums (stoned and cut in half)
110g or 4 oz citron (cut into thin slices)
110g or 4 oz candied peel (cut into thin slices)
1 tsp mixed spice
Half a grated nutmeg
2 tsp salt
450g or 1 lb breadcrumbs
450g or 1 lb sifted flour
450g or 1 lb eggs weighed in their shells
A wineglass of brandy
Half a pint of milk

Method

'Beat the eggs to a froth, and then add to them half a pint of new milk and mix the various ingredients. Let the mixture stand for 12 hours in a cool place, and then put in moulds and boil for eight hours. Three ordinary sized puddings can be made by any culinary member of a family from the aforementioned recipe.'

Daily Chronicle, 1911

The Victorian Era

In 1865 the estate was bought by John Clowes who is described in the then current edition of *Who's Who in Herefordshire* as 'a country gentleman interested in public and social activities in the neighbourhood of his home.' In 1872 he established a reading-room library known as The Burton Court Lending Library in the village. Members paid one penny weekly to gain access to the daily and weekly papers, monthly periodicals and books.

A great feast was held when his son returned from the Boer War and took up residence with his wife and young son in 1885. Shortly afterwards Burton Court entered upon what may be termed its hey day, between 1902 and 1914.

During this time the 'indoor' staff consisted of a butler, three pantrymen, two footmen and a hallboy, a housekeeper, three housemaids, a cook, kitchen maid, scullery maid, pot boy and the lady's maid. The 'outdoor' staff comprised the head gardener, two gardeners, a head groom and two under grooms, a stable boy, laundry maid, head gamekeeper and under gamekeeper. There was also an estate carpenter, much of whose work is still visible in the Court.

The head groom received a free cottage and 26 shillings a week, with free skimmed milk, manure for his garden and £5 of coal a year; the head gardener received similar benefits, but with free vegetables replacing the skimmed milk and manure. Every Christmas the head groom, head gardener and the butler were presented with two shirts and 10 shillings as a Christmas box.

In addition to the brougham horses, between eight and twelve hunters and hacks were kept. There was also the farm stock, which after the death of Master Clowes in France in 1918, were mainly black—Berkshire pigs, black sheep and Welsh cattle. These were managed by the farm staff which included the bailiff, waggoner, cowman and farm boy. The home farm supplied the kitchens, where the bacon was smoked.

The servants' eating hall, now a workshop, was where all the servants in their black livery were summoned for three meals a day by the bell in the clocktower. After the main course everyone stood up whilst the butler, housekeeper, lady's maid and cook retired to the housekeeper's room, or pudding room, as it was called; the rest remaining in the servants' hall.

Mary Edwards, a third housemaid at Burton Court, now in her 80's wrote to me from Australia where she now lives. 'There used to be a stampede at lunchtime. Rogers, the butler, carved the meat which was then passed to cook at the far end of the table to dish out the vegetables. I can assure you it wasn't very hot by the time 'Grace' was said. Then after the meat course the senior members of staff paraded back to the Pudding Room at the far end of the passage.'

I had heard tales of a Pudding Room at Burton Court, but Pamela Horn's introduction to *The Complete Servant* (written in 1825 by Samuel and Sarah Adams, and recently republished by Southover Press) first indicated that this could have been a true story. She confirms that upper servants only ate their main course in the servants hall, then retiring to the housekeeper's room or steward's room to eat their pudding. Irreverent juniors sometimes nicknamed the room Pug's Parlour.

Mary Edwards also remembers having to wash the tiled floor of the conservatory every day with a pail of milk from the dairy. She writes that 'through all my service years I realised I had an excellent training at Burton Court, and would come back again and clean the Gun Room floor and scrub all the front steps.'

Much of the Clowes family dinner service still remains, though reduced in extent over the years. Recently, whilst carrying out repair work we found an old cup bearing the Clowes crest concealed behind a wall in a maid's bedroom. The handle had been broken off, and the cup successfully concealed from the family for all those years, and more.

With so many cookery books now on sale there was a wide choice of menu for the hostess. Two of the most successful cookery writers of the day were Eliza Acton and Isabella Beeton. Poetess Eliza Acton's *Modern Cookery for Private Families* was first published in 1845 and reached its fourteenth edition by 1854, unlike her poems which didn't sell. In 1861 and at the age of 25, Isabella Beeton published her mammoth work *The Book of Household Management*, which firmly established itself as an all time classic.

This Victorian era, with all its soirées and 'At Homes' in the Great Hall, was the age of puddings, raised pies and the regular use of jelly moulds. The puddings received titles such as Prince Albert's, Cabinet or Chancellor's Pudding, Lemon Wonder and Poor Knights of Windsor Pudding.

Despite the names the food was basically plain, wholesome and nourishing, as my great grandmother's recipes show. It was not until 1889 when the great French chef Escoffier arrived at London's new Savoy Hotel that the English were introduced to the wonders of the grand cuisine.

Stilton and Walnut Flan

This recipe of mine is for a delicious yuletide flan—especially when you h.
stilton cheese to hand.

Ingredients for the pastry (Serves 6)
225g or 8 oz plain flour
55g or 2 oz butter
55g or 2 oz lard
1 level tsp salt
Appx. 4 tbs cold water to mix

For the filling
1 large onion
25g or 1 oz butter
170g or 6oz blue stilton cheese
85g or 3 oz roasted and chopped walnuts
   (freshly shelled)
3 eggs
Half tbs port or madeira (optional)
150ml or 5 fl oz milk
60ml or 2 and a half fl oz single cream
Salt & pepper

Method
Sift the flour and salt in a bowl.

Add the fats cut into small pieces and rub in with the finger tips until the mixture resembles fine breadcrumbs.

Add sufficient water to mix to a firm pliable dough, using a round-bladed knife or a form. Knead lightly and chill the dough.

Line a 9 inch flan tin with the pastry and bake blind in a 400°F, 200°C or gas mark 6 oven for 10 minutes.

Melt the butter and place the finely sliced chopped onion in it and fry gently until golden brown.

Crumble the stilton into a bowl and beat in the eggs with a fork. Add the milk, cream, the port or madeira and seasonings.

Spread the onions and walnuts over the pastry base, pour on the cheese mixture and return to the oven for a further 30 minutes or until the filling has set. Serve hot.

A Victorian Salad Dressing

This is an excellent oil free salad dressing which keeps for many weeks, and does not need to be kept in a refrigerator.

Ingredients
1 and half level dsp of table salt
2 level dsp of mustard powder
2 level dsp plain flour
4 heaped dsp caster sugar
2 eggs
300ml or half pt milk
150ml or quarter pt white vinegar

Method
Mix all the dry ingredients together, then work in the eggs.
Add milk to the mixture, then the vinegar.
On a low heat bring slowly up to the boil stirring frequently with a wooden spoon. Do not let it boil.
As the mixture cools it will thicken more.
Keep in screw top jars.

Raspberry Vinegar Cordial

This recipe comes from my husband's grandmother's recipe notebook. Our sons enjoy this cordial with plenty of ice and soda.

Ingredients
1.8kg or 4lbs raspberries
1.1 litres or 2 pts white wine vinegar or white distilled vinegar
550g or 1 and a quarter pounds preserving sugar to each pint of juice

Method
Bruise the raspberries lightly and put them in an earthenware or china bowl with the vinegar.
Cover and leave to stand for four days, stirring every day.
Strain through a jelly-bag or fine cloth.
Measure the juice and add the sugar. Stir over a low heat until the sugar is dissolved, then boil rapidly for 15 minutes, stirring well.
Cool and bottle.
To serve, put 2 to 3 tablespoons of raspberry vinegar to a glass of ice and soda water.

Venison Steaks in Christopher North's Sauce

Venison is inclined to be dry and hard unless carefully cooked. Fresh supplies can be found in the larger supermarkets except during three weeks in July, and some local game and fishmongers can supply it.

It is not necessary to marinate young doe, but it may be so for red deer venison. The Roman Apicius manuscript gives a delicious selection of sauces for venison, and an excellent marinade for pot roasting with spices, honey, dates and raisins. The sauce I have selected is by Christopher North, a professor of moral philosophy at Edinburgh, and is taken from Eliza Acton's *Modern Cookery for Private Families* published in 1845.

Ingredients (Serves 4)
4 venison steaks appx. 2.5cm or 1 inch thick, 170g or 6 oz each.
   (From the best end or loin)
2 tbs olive oil
2 to 3 tbs port, wine or stock
Watercress to garnish

For the sauce
2 tbs Harvey's Sauce (see page 57) or
   2 tsp malt vinegar
   2 tsp walnut ketchup or walnut pickle juice
   3 anchovy fillets (pre-soaked in milk, and pounded)
   1 crushed garlic clove
   Half a shallot, finely chopped
1 tbs lemon juice
2 tsp mushroom ketchup
1 glass port wine
2 tsp caster sugar
Heaped saltspoon cayenne pepper
Half tsp salt

Method
Remove every piece of skin and fat from the steaks. Season with pepper and beat out the steaks lightly.

Heat the oil in a frying pan until very hot, and then cook the steaks very fast for 2 minutes on each side. Remove the steaks to a warm serving dish, and add the port, wine or stock to the pan juices. Heat and pour over the steaks.

In a basin mix together the sugar, salt and cayenne. Add by degrees the rest of the ingredients. Mix well. Place the basin over a pan of boiling water and heat to almost boiling, but do not let it boil.

Serve in a separate sauceboat and dish up the venison garnished with the watercress. Eliza Acton suggests you can add this quantity of sauce to 450ml or three-quarters pint of strong thick brown gravy. Rowan or redcurrant jelly is traditionally served with venison.

My Victorian great-grandmother Julia Lewin's recipes

Julia Dickens entered the service of the Knightley family of Fawsley Hall in Northamptonshire, rising to become head laundress. Whilst she was there she met and fell in love with John Lewin, a yeoman farmer who farmed in the valley below at Badby. They were married at Rushden Church on 31 March 1865, moved to a farm at Cogenhoe and then, in 1895, took up a tenancy of Avenue Farm at Yardley Hastings on the Marquess of Northampton's Castle Ashby estate.

Her granddaughter Frances, now in her 90th year, was brought up at Avenue Farm and can remember Julia Lewin fashioning butter sculptures for the marquess's table at the castle. Swans with cygnets and wild dog roses were rushed on ice by pony and trap to his kitchen.

Sadly she was widowed just three months after taking up the tenancy, and so set about farming the land herself with the aid of her son Richard. She turned the farmhouse with its eleven bedrooms into a guest house, and London gentlemen arrived for shooting parties, to be escorted by her son on pheasant and deer shoots. Food was abundant, and maids, nursemaids, a boot boy and gardener were employed, some of them living in.

It was a hard life organising the farm labourers, rearing chickens, making butter, organising the eggs and butter to be sent to Northampton Market, dealing with callers for their halfpenny pint of skimmed milk, and with dogs, cats and lambs to care for. But amongst all this she managed to produce some very fine fare.

Frances recalls special occasions when senior members of the marquess's staff, including the butler and head gardener, would arrive for one of Julia's dinner parties at which everyone was required to dress in their very best clothes, including the grandchildren. She recalls the head footman, Mr. Norton, accidently keeling over on his chair exclaiming 'Oh Mrs. Lewin, your wonderful hare soup again.'

Fortunately some of the Yardley Hastings recipes have survived, and a selection are given below. As game was so plentiful, raised pies were a favourite, in which she usually used wild mushrooms. These added a special flavour when cold, but I find they have no keeping power. And, of course, an all butter crust was a must.

Avenue Farm Pork and Ham Pies

pies were made at a time, using 7 lbs of flour and 3 pints of milk from
.pe is more modest, and I have added some chopped ham which gives a
.aste to the little pies. Eggs boiled for 7 minutes can also be placed inside

gredients for the hot water crust (Serves 8 from 4 medium pies)

450g or 1 lb strong white plain flour
1 tsp salt
1 tbs icing sugar
2 beaten eggs
75g or 2 and a half oz butter
75g or 2 and a half oz lard
200ml or 7 fl oz milk or water

For the filling

350g or 12 oz lean pork, coarsely minced or cubed
8 oz or 225g ham, cubed small
1 tsp chopped sage
1 tbs chopped parsley
1 tsp anchovy essence (optional)
Half tsp each grated nutmeg, ground cloves, allspice
Rind and juice of half a lemon
Salt and pepper
1 tbs brandy
A little butter

For the savoury jelly

1 pig's trotter
1 bay leaf
1 onion
1 carrot
6 peppercorns
2 tsp bovril or marmite

Method

Prepare the jelly the day before. Boil the washed trotter, bay leaf, carrot, onion and peppercorns in 600ml or 1 pint of water for about 3 hours.

Strain the liquid into a basin and leave overnight. A quarter of a pint will be sufficient for the pies.

Prepare the filling: Trim the excess fat and gristle off the pork and dice into 2 inch cubes. Toss in the seasonings, then put through a coarse mincer, or cube smaller. Add the cubed ham and the rest of the ingredients including the brandy and mix well. Set aside.

Make the pastry: Sift the flour, salt and icing sugar in a bowl. Make a deep well in the middle into which you pour the beaten eggs. Toss a little flour over the eggs.

Melt the butter and lard slowly in the milk or water. Once it has boiled pour it quickly over the flour, mixing with a knife.

Knead until the pastry is smooth, then wrap in polythene and refrigerate for 15 minutes.

Reserve a quarter of the pastry for the lids and keep it wrapped. Divide the rest into four and roll out and mould around four wetted and well floured 1 lb jam jars.

Chill until the pastry is firm, about 20 minutes, then carefully remove the jars.

Stand the cases on a baking sheet and spoon in the prepared minced filling, filling the cases well and place a small nob of butter on the top of each pie.

Divide the remaining quarter of the pastry into four, and roll out circles to fit the tops of the pies. Wet the sides and seal and crimp where pastry joins the edges. Do not make a hole in them and with a little beaten egg place a few pastry leaves on top for decoration. Tie a double sided sheet of greased greaseproof paper around each pie, securing with paper clips top and bottom, to prevent the sides from bulging.

Bake in a moderate oven for 1 hour 30 minutes, 325°F, 170°C or gas mark 3. After one and a quarter hours remove greaseproof supports, brush sides and top with a beaten egg and salt glaze. Return to the oven for the last 15 minutes.

Remove from the oven and allow to get almost cool on a wire rack.

Make a small hole in each pie. Warm the jelly adding half a teaspoon of marmite or bovril. Using a small funnel gradually pour the jelly through to the meat. Keep topping up and leave them to cool and set.

Harvey's Sauce

This sauce is named after Peter Harvey, the publican of The George in Bedford. Stopping at the inn one day a Captain Charles Combers had produced his own sauce bottle after ordering a steak, leaving the remaining contents of the bottle for Harvey's use. Harvey soon found his other customers liked the sauce and later obtained the recipe from the Captain, who in turn had had it from his mother. There are several variations, this one comes from *The Compleat Servant Maid*, published in 1677. The sauce improves after a year's keeping.

Ingredients

12 filleted anchovies	1 and a half bulbs garlic
1 tsp cayenne pepper	1 tsp cochineal
Half tbs mushroom ketchup	1 shallot
5 tsp walnut pickle juice or walnut ketchup	2.25 litres or 4 pints vinegar

Method

Pound the anchovies, add the pepper, mushroom ketchup and walnut juice.

Chop the garlic heads, add the cochineal and chopped shallot. Add the vinegar and stand for 14 days. Stir well twice or thrice a day, then strain it till quite clear. Bottle.

Julia Lewin's Raised Pheasant & Ham Pie

Ingredients for the hot water crust pastry (Serves appx. 8)

675g or 1 and a half lbs strong white plain flour
1 and a half tsp salt
3 beaten eggs
300ml or 10 fl oz water
115g or 4 oz butter
100g or 3 and a half oz lard

For the forcemeat

450g or 1 lb chopped veal or belly pork
Half tsp salt (if using veal)
Pinch of cayenne pepper
Ground pepper
Quarter tsp ground mace
Half tsp freshly grated nutmeg

Half tsp ground allspice
Rind of one lemon
Juice from half a lemon
2 tbs chopped parsley
1 tbs freshly chopped sage
1 egg

The breasts of a brace of pheasants
(approximately 450g or 1lb)
225g or 8 oz sliced ham
600ml or 1 pint savoury jelly

Method

Butter a 9 inch oblong fluted pie mould, or a deep 8 inch spring clip cake tin.

As for the recipe for Avenue Farm Pork & Ham Pies make up the hot water pastry, making sure that the water and fat heats up slowly and the water does not evaporate.

Line the pastry mould, leaving a quarter clear for the lid and decorations. Keep covered.

Cut the pheasant meat into pieces, and season well with ground pepper, salt and a little ground mace.

Mix all the forcemeat ingredients together well.

Spread a layer of the prepared forcemeat in the bottom of the pastry case, then a layer of the seasoned pheasant, then the slices of ham. Repeat to the top of the pie case, packing tight to the sides and leaving a dome shape in the middle to keep the pie well up.

Wet the edges of the pie and lay the cover on top and crimp well together. Brush with egg white, and plait some pastry round the edges and decorate with pastry leaves. Leave a pie funnel hole in the centre.

Brush again with egg white. Bake in a moderate oven 170°C, 325°F or gas mark 3 for 2 hours. Cover with greaseproof paper or brown paper if over browning on top.

After 1 hour 30 minutes brush again with beaten egg and 1 teaspoon of salt to give a good glaze. When almost completely cooled down, poor enough warmed savoury jelly, flavoured with 1 tablespoon of madeira or 1 teaspoon of bovril, through the hole.

Leave to cool and slice as required.

Julia Lewin's You and Me Loaf

Buttermilk straight from the dairy was used in cakes and scones at Avenue Farm—it gives a wonderful flavour. This loaf is good sliced and buttered for afternoon tea.

Ingredients

450g or 1 lb self raising flour
225g or 8 oz ordinary sugar
225g or 8 oz sultanas
2 tbs treacle
300ml or half pint buttermilk (or full cream milk)
1 egg
Half tsp grated nutmeg

Method

Mix all the dry ingredients together.
Beat in the beaten egg, milk and melted treacle and mix well together.
Bake in a slow oven for 1 hour 30 minutes, 325°F, 160°C or gas mark 3.

Eliza Acton's Forced Eggs for garnishing salads

This recipe is taken from *Modern Cookery for Private families* published in 1845.

Ingredients

6 eggs
4 anchovies
Butter, size of two yolks
Quarter tsp mace
Cayenne, third as much

Method

Pound and press through the back of a hair-sieve the flesh of three very fine, or four moderate-sized anchovies, freed from the bones and skin. Boil six fresh eggs for twelve minutes, and when they are perfectly cold halve them lengthwise, take out the yolks, pound them to a paste with a third of their volume of fresh butter, then add the anchovies, a quarter of a teaspoonful of mace, and as much cayenne as will season the mixture well; beat these together thoroughly, and fill the whites of eggs neatly with them. A morsel of garlic, perfectly blended with the other ingredients, would to some tastes improve this preparation: a portion of anchovy butter, or of potted ham, will supply the places of fish in it very advantageously.

Julia Lewin's Velvet Pudding

Whilst Julia Lewin called her recipe Velvet Pudding, there appear to be several recipes for Velvet Cream in early recipe books. By the Edwardian era it appears as a sherried cream blanc-mange. Covered on top with halved almonds it turned into a Hedgehog Pudding! The following recipe is best served ice-cold.

Ingredients (Serves 6)
425ml or three-quarters pint milk
150ml or quarter pint double cream
A few drops vanilla or almond essence
50g or 2 oz ground rice
25g or 1 oz caster sugar
25g or 1 oz fresh butter
Rind of half a lemon
1 tbs good sweet sherry
A few fresh raspberries, or halved almonds for a garnish
    (optional)
A little raspberry jam

Method
Boil the milk and cream and add a few drops of vanilla essence.

Gradually whisk in the ground rice. Bring back to the boil and gently simmer for 10 minutes, until cooked, stirring frequently.

Add the sugar and beat in the butter, lemon rind and add the sherry.

Place the jam in a glass dish, cover with the above mixture and cool.

When ice-cold pipe rosettes of cream and garnish with a few fresh raspberries. Place halved almonds all over the top to represent hedgehog spikes.

Black Cherry Velvet Cream

Using almond essence follow the recipe as above for stages 1 and 2. At stage 3 omit the sherry and substitute one tablespoon of Kirsch or Cherry Brandy. Place some black cherry jam at the bottom of tall sundae glasses and cover with a layer of the mixture and then a few pitted black cherries, and repeat to the top of the glass, finishing with the ground rice. Garnish with whipped cream, grated dark chocolate, and a few frosted pitted black cherries tossed in egg white and caster sugar.

Some Family Recipes

I can't abear a Butcher,
    I can't abide his meat
The ugliest shop of all is his,
    The ugliest in the street;
Bakers' are warm, cobblers' dark,
    Chemists' burn watery lights;
But oh, the sawdust butcher's shop
    That ugliest of sights!

                    Walter de la Mare

I grew up during the war years in the heart of Hereford and the sights, smells, and sounds are still vivid in my memory. We lived above my mother's two shops in the middle of Eign Street, where Woolworths now stands. A butchery shop had been acquired by her first husband who died young, leaving her to bring up her family in her late twenties. She began to expand and acquired the shop next door which she turned into a delicatessen specialising in cooked meats. At the back of the premises she built a pork pie bakery and sausage making enterprise employing thirty people and where sausages and pies were turned out by the score to supply the local hospitals, canteens and schools.

Wednesday, as now, was market day and the town bustled with farmers and their wives. One old farmer regularly came into the cooked meats shop demanding 'Give us two of them tu'penny pies. What's in 'em?'

At the top of Eign Street is the High Street, on which lay Evans's Beauty Parlour where you could be 'strung up' to the newest Eugene hair wave. Further along was Marchant's Grocery where one savoured the smell of roasting coffee that drifted through a mesh hole out into the street. There was also the joy and pleasure of putting a penny in the singing bird caged down in the basement toy department of Hereford's largest emporium, Greenlands, which stood where Marks and Spencers is now. At the other end of High Town was 'The Furriers of the West', Augustus Edwards, with its magnificent curved fronted windows. Displayed on the stairs leading to the fur department mezzanine floor were a host of snarling stuffed natural history specimens, including leopards, ocelots, squirrels and otters. In the autumn there was the aroma of the apples being pressed at the Bulmers cider works which seemed to tower over the city. Always there was the sound of All Saints Church, and the great tolling bells of the cathedral.

As one of five daughters, my mother instilled upon us that 'if we couldn't do anything else in life, we must at least be able to cook.' Away from the worries of the business, cooking was her relaxation. The stockpot invariably on the go, she produced some fine fare with enthusiasm. Over the years she built up a library of cookery books from all over the world and avidly followed the cookery writers of her day.

Mother's Boiled Beef and Carrots

This was one of our favourites.

Ingredients (Serves 8)

1.8 to 2.3kg or 4 to 5 lbs salt beef
    (or silverside tied firmly with string)
675 to 900g or 1 and a half to 2 lbs carrots
3 or 4 peeled spanish onions
3 or 4 peeled turnips
Bouquet garni (parsley, thyme, bay leaves)
A few peppercorns

For the herb dumplings
115g or 4 oz self-raising flour
Half tsp salt
50g or 2 oz suet
Water to mix
1 tbs parsley, chives or mixed herbs
    (I use fresh marjoram and parsley)

Method

If the beef is still salty, soak it overnight, then place it in a large saucepan with any bones the butcher may have offered you.

Cover it with cold water and bring it slowly to the boil.

Add half of the vegetables and the bouquet garni and peppercorns. Cover and simmer gently for 2 to 3 hours, longer if the meat is tough.

Meanwhile make the dumplings: Sieve the flour and salt in a bowl.

Blend in the suet with a knife. Stir in enough water to bind the mixture until it is soft enough to divide into eight portions and roll into balls with floured hands.

Returning to the beef, add more water if the liquid is too salty.

During the last 25 to 30 minutes cook the rest of the vegetables and add the prepared dumplings, which must be cooked for at least 20 minutes.

Serve the beef with the freshly cooked vegetables and dumplings, and some of the broth. Keep the rest of the stock for a wonderful soup base.

Knights of St. John Pie

Clockwise from bottom left: You and Me Loaf, Dinner rolls,
Poppy Seed Plait and Burton Court Brown Bread, Christmas Stollen Loaf

Good King Henry's Plait

Wye Salmon Mousse and Flan

From left to right: Avenue Farm Pork and Ham Pies,
Raised Pheasant & Ham Pie, Raspberry Vinegar Cordial

Granny's Boiled Batter Pudding

Traditionally this pudding was served with the roast meat on sundays. I remember my grandmother serving this dish as a first course with a slice of butter and plenty of brown sugar, and relished every mouthful—as did the eldest grandchild who had had to beat the batter by hand for half an hour. It filled us up and so economised on the meat rations. I often add powdered ginger and chopped stem ginger to the basic recipe given here.

Ingredients (Serves 7 to 8)
600ml or 1 pint milk
225g or 8 oz flour
6 eggs
Half a level tsp salt
Quarter tsp freshly grated nutmeg

Method
Sift the flour, salt and nutmeg. Beat in the eggs gradually with the milk and mix to a smooth paste.

Tie the mixture in a floured cloth or put into a buttered 2 pint basin and cover with greaseproof paper, then tie a cloth over the top.

Boil for between 2 hours 30 minutes to 3 hours. Serve with butter and brown sugar.

Mother's Carrot Pudding

Ingredients (Serves 4 to 6)

170g or 6 oz seedless raisins, chopped
A little sweet Herefordshire cider
170g or 6 oz butter
225g or 8 oz carrots, peeled and grated
140g or 5 oz flour
1 tsp baking powder

Half tsp salt
170g or 6 oz soft brown sugar
Half tsp grated nutmeg
Half tsp powdered cinnamon
1 tbs lemon juice

Method
Soak the raisins overnight in the cider then strain the raisins and discard the cider.
Cream the butter and stir in the raisins and carrots.
Sift the flour, baking powder and salt and mix with the remaining ingredients.
Work into the carrot mixture and press into a shallow baking dish.
Bake in a very moderate oven, 350°F, 180°C or gas mark 3 for about 40 minutes. Sprinkle with a little caster sugar and serve. It's especially delicious if served with cream.

Carrots were introduced as a vegetable to England from Flanders in the Elizabethan era. The late André Simon wrote that attempts to use carrots as fruit, in puddings, have been failures, but then perhaps he had not tried this Herefordshire carrot pudding!

Granny's Brandied Seed Cake

In the latter part of the eighteenth century caraway seeds were enormously popular. In 1769 Mrs. Elizabeth Raffald published 800 original recipes in her book *The Experienced English Housekeeper,* one of which was a rich seed cake in which she recommends beating the cake for two hours and folding in the egg whites separately. But then she had plenty of help in the kitchen for she gave birth to no less than fifteen daughters. My grandmother's recipe is less arduous, and she always included some brandy.

Ingredients
285g or 10 oz unsalted butter, softened
285g or 10 oz caster sugar
140g or 5 oz plain flour
140g or 5 oz cornflour
4 size 2 eggs, separated
50ml or 3 tbs brandy
30ml or 1 and a half tbs milk
25g or 1 oz caraway seeds
1 tsp grated nutmeg
1 tsp cinnamon

Method
Cream the butter until pale, then gradually add the sugar.

Sift the flour and cornflour together, and add a spoonful to the butter cream before breaking in the beaten egg yolks.

Beat well, and continue in the same manner until all the ingredients (except the egg whites) are used up, adding the brandy and milk as you go.

Lastly beat up the egg whites and fold these in gradually with a cutting movement.

Bake in a lined and greased 8 inch cake or Pullman tin in a moderate oven, 325°F, 170°C or gas mark 3 for 1 hour 30 minutes.

Cool in the tin.

Granny's Walnut Cider Cake

Ingredients

115g or 4 oz butter
115g or 4 oz sugar
2 eggs
55g or 2 oz chopped walnuts
225g or 8 oz plain flour
1 tsp bicarbonate of soda
1 tsp grated nutmeg
1 teacupful of cider

For the filling
25g or 1 oz butter
1 dsp soya flour or grated nuts
85g or 3 oz dates
2 tbs honey
Squeeze of lemon juice

Method

Beat the butter and sugar to a cream, add the eggs well beaten, walnuts, and then half the flour sifted with the soda and nutmeg.

Pour over the cider, beat to a froth and mix thoroughly. Stir in the remainder of the flour, turn into a shallow well greased tin and bake for 45 minutes in a moderate oven, 350°F, 180°C or gas mark 4.

For the filling, cream the butter thoroughly, add the soya flour or grated nuts, dates and honey and squeeze of lemon juice.

Split the cake into three when cold and sandwich with the filling. Dust with some icing sugar, or use a white icing glaze and add a few halved walnuts along the top.

Granny's Blackcurrant Pie

I have added some chopped mint to my grandmother's recipe as I do with all my blackcurrant dishes; a hint of mint seems to complement the blackcurrant flavour. This is delicious served with a home-made egg custard.

Ingredients for the flaky pastry (for a 20cm or 8 inch pie dish)

225g or 8 oz plain flour
Half tsp salt
140g or 5 oz butter or butter and lard mixed
Half tsp lemon juice
Appx. 150ml or quarter pint cold water to mix

For the filling
225g or 8 oz blackcurrants
115g or 4 oz caster sugar
2 heaped tablespoons finely chopped mint

Icing sugar for dusting

Method

Mix the salt with the flour and sift into a bowl.

Divide the fat into four parts, and rub one quarter into the flour. Add the lemon juice and enough water to mix to an elastic dough.

Roll into a long strip on a floured board, three times as long as it is wide. Spread another quarter of the fat, cut into small pieces, two-thirds of the way down the pastry, leaving a third uncovered and retaining a margin of half an inch at the sides.

Fold the uncovered part of the pastry up over a covered third, then the remaining covered third down over the folded pastry. Seal the edges and 'rib' with a rolling pin across the pastry at regular intervals—this helps to distribute the air evenly. Put in a polythene bag and chill for 15 minutes.

Remove the pastry from the refrigerator and, with the folded side of the pastry to the right, roll out again to a strip three times as long as it is wide. Repeat the 'flaking' process with the second portion of fat, fold as before and chill again for 15 minutes.

Repeat as above using the final portion of fat, then do a further rolling and folding process without adding any fat. Chill for about 1 hour, after which it is ready to use.

Roll out the chilled pastry to the required shape, reserving any trimmings for pastry leaves.

Place the fruit, sugar and chopped mint into the bottom of the pie dish, place a funnel support in the centre and place the rolled out pastry on top, denting the sides and decorate with pastry leaves. Brush the pastry with a beaten egg and a sprinkling of caster sugar. Bake in a very hot oven for 10 minutes, 425°F, 220°C or gas mark 7, then turn down the oven to 325°F, 170°C or gas mark 3 for a further 30 minutes.

Just before serving, dust with icing sugar.

Mother's Orange Madeira Cake

A very rich and good keeping cake.

Ingredients

175g or 6 and a half oz butter
175g or 6 and a half oz caster sugar
6 eggs
350g or 12 oz plain flour
Pinch of salt
2 tsp baking powder
Zest of an orange
60ml or 3 and a half tbs double cream
60ml or 3 and a half tbs orange juice
2 tsp orange essence
Few slices of orange candied peel

Method

Cream the butter and sugar together well.

Beat in the eggs one by one with a little flour per egg.

Add the orange zest, cream, orange juice and orange essence. Mix in the sifted flour, salt and baking powder.

Place in a greased and floured 8 inch tin, or Pullman tin.

Bake in a moderate oven for 1 hour 15 minutes, 350°F, 180°C or gas mark 4. Half way through the cooking time and once the cake feels set, add the slices of orange peel to the top. (If you do this at the outset of cooking, the peel is inclined to sink.)

Candied Citrus Peel

If you want to make your own candied peel, cut the peel of two oranges (preferably ripe, but not over ripe) into strips, cover with cold water and bring to the boil slowly, boiling until tender.

Make a syrup with 115g or 4 oz of sugar and 4 tablespoons of water. Drop the peel in and boil until nearly all is absorbed and the peel is nearly tansparent.

Dry slowly in the sun or a warm, not hot, oven. The peel should be crystalline when quite dry.

Mother's Shortbreads

Ingredients
225g or 8 oz plain flour
55g or 2 oz cornflour
Half tsp salt
55g or 2 oz ground rice
115g or 4 oz caster sugar
225g or 8 oz butter

Method
Sift the flour, cornflour and salt.

Add the ground rice and sugar.

Rub in the butter until you have fine breadcrumbs, then form into a ball and roll out. Cut into 3 inch rounds and prick with a fork.

Bake for 20 minutes at 375°F, 190°C, or gas mark 5.

Oat Biscuits for Cheese

I make these in batches, as they deep freeze well.

Ingredients (Makes 12)
115g or 4 oz fine oatmeal
85g or 3 oz plain rye flour
Half tsp baking powder
Half tsp salt
45g or 1 and a half oz lard or beef dripping
50ml or 3 tbs cold water

Method
Put the oatmeal into a basin and sieve on to it the flour, baking powder and salt.

Rub in the lard or dripping and mix to a stiff dough with the water.

Knead lightly then roll out thinly on a floured board. Cut into 3 and a half inch (8.5cm) rounds and prick all over with a fork.

Put on a greased baking sheet and bake in a 400°F, 200°C gas mark 6 oven for 12 minutes, until the biscuits are pale brown.

Spread on a wire rack to cool.

Today's Recipes

'A man is in general better pleased when he has a good dinner upon his table, than when his wife talks Greek.' Samuel Johnson.

In 1949 an era ended at Burton Court with the death of Mrs. Clowes, her son already having been killed during the First World War. Up to the end she managed to maintain a small staff, but the only link I have with this past is the head coachman's granddaughter, Pat. As head coachman he was sent to Yeovil to learn to drive one of the first motor cars to be seen in the county. Her father was to serve as valet and her mother as Mrs. Clowes' secretary.

During the 1950's, when all the supporting farms of the 1,000 acre estate were sold, the Court became something of a white elephant, until my husband came out of the navy and rescued it for use as a residence and soft fruit growing enterprise. In 1972 we were married and I became the new 'mistress' of Burton Court! For my husband it has been a love affair with a building, gradually restoring and nurturing it.

Cream of Chestnut Soup

My husband believes the sweet chestnut trees flanking the entrance to our drive to be at least 350 years old and I ponder that many a cook down the centuries concocted recipes using the chestnuts—so long as they could gather them before the squirrels!

Ingredients (Serves 4)
450g or 1 lb fresh chestnuts
600ml or 1 pint good chicken stock
55g or 2 oz margarine or butter
300ml or half a pint milk
Half tsp salt
Freshly grated nutmeg
Half tsp sugar

Method
Score the skins of the chestnuts. Cover with water and cook for 20 minutes.

Peel the nuts and inner skins whilst still warm and put the chestnuts into the stock. Simmer gently for 45 minutes.

Rub the chestnuts through a sieve or liquidize.

Return to the pan together with the margarine or butter, milk, seasonings and sugar.

Heat slowly and serve with croutons, which I like to toss in coarse dried garlic. Finally garnish with a little grated nutmeg.

Madeira Minced Beef Pie

'A good meal ought to begin with hunger.' French Proverb.

Mrs. Leyel's popular cookery book *The Gentle Art of Cookery* was first published in 1925. I have adapted this basic minced beef and raisin recipe of hers into a richer potato topped pie. This sustaining winter dish can be kept hot and unspoilt whilst waiting for guests to arrive.

Ingredients (Serves 6 to 8)
450g or 1 lb lean minced beef
115g or 4 oz sultanas
3 tbs madeira or red wine
450g or 1 lb chestnuts
2 medium onions
2 garlic cloves
1 tbs olive oil
25g or 1 oz butter
175g or 7 oz canned chopped tomatoes
25g or 1 oz flour
600ml or 1 pint brown stock
1 tsp bovril
6 cloves, crushed
3 tbs chopped parsley
1 dsp lemon juice

For the topping
1kg or 2 and a quarter lbs red potatoes
2 egg yolks
55g or 2 oz butter or margarine
Half tsp grated nutmeg
A little melted butter for glaze
Coarse oatmeal or crushed cornflakes

Method
Soak the sultanas in the madeira overnight.

Score and boil the chestnuts for 10 minutes. Skin them and chop finely or put them through a coarse mincer.

Peel the onions and garlic and chop finely. Fry them gently, not browning them, in the olive oil and butter for 3 minutes.

Add the chopped tomatoes and cook for a further 2 minutes. Gradually stir in the flour away from the heat, and return to cook over a low heat stirring all the time. Slowly add the brown stock and bovril. Bring to the boil and cook until slightly thickened.

Add the meat, minced chestnuts and crushed cloves, stirring well to break up the meat.

Season to taste and cook over a low heat in a covered saucepan for 30 minutes, stirring occasionally.

Boil the potatoes, mash them and add the grated nutmeg, egg yolks and melted butter. Beat well and season.

Add the madeira, soaked sultanas, parsley and lemon juice to the meat sauce, and place in a shallow pie dish.

Place three-quarters of the duchess potatoes on top using the remainder for piping rosettes around the dish. Brush with a little melted butter and sprinkle some coarse oatmeal or crushed cornflakes over the top.

Bake in an oven at 180°C, 350°F or gas mark 4 for 30 minutes until golden brown.

Chestnut Cake

This sandwich cake can be filled with apricot jam and the top glazed with a sieved reduced apricot jam, or filled with strawberry jam and cream, or iced with chocolate and filled with whipped cream and chopped nuts.

Ingredients
225g or 9 oz chestnuts, weighed when cooked and sieved
  (appx. 12 oz unpeeled)
4 eggs
100g or 3 and half oz butter
125g or 4 and half oz caster sugar
1 tsp Vanilla essence

Method
Grease and well flour a swiss roll tin.

To cook the chestnuts, first peel them and then scald in boiling water to remove the inner skin. Then simmer in water until just soft, drain well and push through a wire sieve. The result should be dry and powdery.

Separate the eggs. Put the yolks in a bowl with the sugar and beat for 5 to 6 minutes. Add the vanilla essence.

Melt the butter. Whip the egg whites, fold them into the yolks and sugar with the chestnuts. Before completely mixed, add the melted butter very quickly.

Turn at once into the prepared swiss roll tin and bake for about 20 minutes in a moderate to hot oven, 375°F, 190°C or gas mark 5.

When brown and well risen, remove to cool slightly before turning out.

When cold turn over on to a board, remove paper and divide into three. Sandwich with the required filling to form a brick and finish as suggested above. Serve on a cake board.

A Prayer for Trees
Ye who pass by and would raise your hand against me,
Hearken ere you harm me,
I am the heat on your hearth on the cold, rainy night.
The friendly shade screening you from the summer sun.
And my fruits are refreshing draughts, quenching your thirst as you journey on.
I am the beam that holds your house,
the board of your table, the bed on which you lie,
the door of your homestead, the wood of your cradle,
     and the shell of your coffin.
I am the breadth of kindness, and the flower of beauty.
Ye who pass by, listen to my prayer —
Harm me not.

Anon

Beefsteak and Kidney Pie

This recipe was first published in the USA in Bernard Clayton's *The Complete Book of Pastry* in 1981. It is a firm favourite with my family. The oysters and sherry can give it that touch of luxury, but these are entirely optional.

Ingredients for the rough puff pastry (Serves 6)

400g or 14 oz plain flour
1 tsp salt
170g or 6 oz semi-frozen butter, or half butter and half lard
Quarter tsp lemon juice
75ml or 4 tbs ice water

For the filling
675g or 1 and a half lbs sirloin or braising steak
225g or half lb kidneys, veal or lamb
1 large onion, chopped
2 tbs fresh bacon dripping or butter
Half tsp salt
Quarter tsp pepper
2 tsp Worcestershire sauce
1 tsp finely chopped parsley
1 bay leaf, crumbled
450ml or three-quarters pint beef stock
5 tbs plain flour
225g or 8 oz mushrooms, sliced, or whole if small
1 pt oysters (optional)
3 tbs sherry (optional)
1 egg (for a glaze)
1 tbs milk (for a glaze)

Method

First prepare the puff pastry which can be made the day before and refrigerated. Sift the flour and salt in a large bowl. Add the coarsely grated semi-frozen butter (or butter and lard) and mix them lightly into the flour with a fork. Add the lemon juice and a few drops of water at a time, enough so as to make a firm but not hard dough.

Wrap the dough in greaseproof paper and chill for 20 minutes.

Roll it into a rectangle 6 inches by 24. Fold lengthwise into thirds, as if folding a letter. Turn so that the open end faces you. Roll a second time into a long rectangle. Fold as before and roll a third time. Fold into thirds. Refrigerate for 15 minutes.

Roll and turn the dough three more times—a total of six times. Wrap and chill while the pie ingredients are being prepared.

Cut the beef into half inch cubes. Soak the kidneys in a bowl of cold water for 30 minutes. Drain and cut away the white fat and cut into half inch pieces. Set aside.

Sauté the chopped onion in bacon dripping over a medium heat until translucent. Add the steak and kidney pieces and sauté until they are browned. Season with salt and pepper. Stir in the Worcestershire sauce, parsley and bay leaf.

Place all the ingredients in a casserole dish and pour over the beef stock, keeping half a pint of liquid to blend with the flour until the lumps disappear. Return to the pot and mix in.

Place in a low oven, 325°F, 170°C or gas mark 3, for 2 hours, stirring occasionally.

Meanwhile, whilst the meat is cooking, roll out the pastry to fit a 13 inch by 9 inch by 2 inch deep baking dish, allowing an extra 1 inch margin, and keeping some for the sides and top. Cut 2 and a half inch strips from the remaining dough to fit the interior sides of the baking dish, and a piece for the top. Carefully fold the dough for the top and wrap in greaseproof paper and refrigerate. Any left-over dough can be set aside and used to fashion the pastry leaves. Moisten the sides with water and arrange the strips in place, allowing the strips to extend a quarter inch above the sides so that a crimped seal can be made with the top dough. When the dough has stuck to the sides, refrigerate.

When the meat has cooked, remove from the oven and allow to cool for 30 minutes. Turn the oven to 450°F, 230°C or gas mark 7.

Stir in the chopped mushrooms, sherry and oysters.

Pour the meat into the prepared baking dish, add the top piece of pastry and trim to allow a half inch margin. Moisten the edges of the top and side dough and crimp together with the fingers to seal. Cut a hole in the centre to allow steam to escape.

Decorate with pastry leaves, crescents etc. Brush with a beaten egg and milk glaze.

Bake on the middle shelf of the hot oven for 20 minutes until the pastry has risen and is slightly brown. Then reduce the heat to 350°F, 180°C or gas mark 4, for a further 15 minutes.

Serve piping hot!

The Romans were immensely fond of a strong tasting but costly liquid fish pickle called Liquamen or Garum and they used it frequently if sparingly all over their food. Made from the fermenting entrails of fish such as mackerel or anchovies, the gills, intestines and blood were mixed with salt to which was added vinegar, parsley, wine and sweet herbs. Dried in open jars in the sun till the fish parts were liquefied this resulted in a thick sauce, which was bottled after two or three months. It became so popular that it was commercially produced, one of the factories being at Pompeii.

Even today at the Roman School of Cookery in Rome, students are required to produce a fish pickle sauce. A blind tasting is then performed against Worcestershire sauce and students invariably cannot tell the difference. The secret Lee and Perrins formula must be partly based on a certain Roman fish pickle!

Welsh Spring Lamb Noisettes

A main dish using Welsh lamb and Worcestershire sauce. Preferably arrange for the butcher to provide the noisettes by cutting the fillets from a loin of a lamb into one and a half inch slices. The noisettes should have a ribbon of fat fastened around them with a wooden stick.

Ingredients (Serves 4)

8 Lamb noisettes
2 cloves garlic, peeled and slivered (optional)
55g or 2 oz butter
4 tsp Worcestershire sauce
1 tsp bovril or marmite
1 glass of red or Madeira wine
300ml or half a pint brown stock
1 tbs tomato purée
Pinch of rosemary
225g or 8 oz carrots, cut into thin sticks
450g or 1 lb petits pois
Salt & pepper
Watercress for a garnish

Method

Cut a few gashes in the noisettes and insert the slivers of garlic. Season them with salt and freshly ground pepper. Place a knob of butter on top and grill, or shallow fry, for about 6 minutes on both sides, basting occasionally so that they appear brown on the outside and light pink inside.

Sprinkle half a teaspoon of Worcestershire sauce over each noisette and place on a warmed dish in a very low oven.

Whilst the noisettes are grilling or shallow frying, cook the carrots and peas.

Pour the heated stock into the pan juices and add the tomato purée, rosemary, bovril or marmite, wine and a knob of butter. Transfer the sauce into a pan and boil until thick.

Strain the sauce over the noisettes and arrange the vegetables and watercress around the dish. Serve with redcurrant or mint jelly.

Worcester Lamb Croquettes

Here is an easy and delicious way to use up leftover cold lamb.

Ingredients (Serves 6)
350g or 12 oz cold cooked lamb, minced
156g or 5 and a half oz Campbell's condensed chicken soup
2 tsps Worcestershire sauce
225g or 8 oz potatoes, peeled, cooked and creamed
Salt & pepper
Pinch of dried rosemary
50g or 2 oz flour seasoned with salt and pepper
1 large egg, well beaten
Dried breadcrumbs for coating
Deep fat for frying

Method
Put the lamb into a mixing bowl and stir in the undiluted soup, Worcestershire sauce, creamed potatoes, rosemary and seasoning.

Divide the mixture into 6 equal portions and shape them into flat, round croquettes.

Coat each croquette first in the flour, then in the beaten egg and finally in the breadcrumbs so that they are evenly and completely coated.

Heat the deep fat to 360°F, 185°C (when a piece of bread dropped into the hot fat browns in 1 minute) and fry the croquettes until they are golden brown. Drain well on kitchen paper.

Place on a bed of boiled rice, garnish with parsley and serve with a salad or green vegetable.

Beryl's Seafood Paté

Beryl Harrison became a chef to Sir Charles Clore's shoots on his estate in Herefordshire before deciding to teach children with handicaps how to cook. This is a paté of her invention and freezes very well.

Ingredients (Serves 8)
210g or 7 and a half oz canned red or pink salmon
210g or 7 and a half oz canned tuna in oil
115g or 4 oz melted butter
170g or 6 oz white breadcrumbs
Juice and grated rind of 2 lemons
115g or 4 oz prawns
300ml or half a pint single cream
3 tsps anchovy essence
Ground black pepper

Method
Remove the dark skin from the salmon, flake the flesh and mix with the juices in the tin together with the tuna and its oil.

Place the breadcrumbs in a bowl with the melted butter, lemon juice and rind.

Add the fish and the prawns.

Stir in the anchovy essence and cream.

Season and garnish with lemon.

Wye Salmon and Smoked Salmon Mousse

This is a rich recipe and can form part of a festive buffet, or can be served with melba toast as an entrée.

Ingredients (Serves 8 to 10)
225g or 8 oz smoked salmon pieces
225g or 8 oz fresh Wye salmon
2 hard boiled eggs

For the cold béchamel sauce
20g or three-quarters oz butter
20g or three-quarters oz flour
300ml or half pint milk
   (infused from poaching salmon)
1 stalk of fennel
Pinch of Fox's smoked salt
150ml or quarter pint mayonnaise
Scant 3 tsp gelatine
60ml or 3 and a half tbs light stock or water
60ml or 3 and a half tbs cream

For the garnish
2 hard boiled eggs
Black olives
Lemon wedges
1 pt or 575 ml aspic jelly (optional)

Method
Poach the salmon in the milk with a fennel stalk for about 20 minutes. Cool, remove the fish and skin, bone and flake it. Cut the smoked salmon into quarter inch pieces, and chop the eggs finely.

Mix the sauce (refer to page 85 if necessary), smoked salt and mayonnaise together.

Dissolve the gelatine in the stock over a gentle heat and add the sauce with the fish and eggs. Lightly whip the cream and fold into the mixture.

Turn into a soufflé dish or oiled fish mould or individual ramekin dishes and leave to set.

Turn out onto the serving dish.

Decorate with sliced hard boiled eggs and spoon over enough cold aspic to hold it in position. Leave to set and then fill the dish with more aspic broken up, and scatter some black olives. Decorate with lemon wedges.

Chicken with Orange Mayonnaise

Ingredients (Serves 8)
1.5kg or 3 and a half lbs cooked chicken
2 large oranges
300ml or half a pint mayonnaise (home-made if possible)
50ml or 3tbs orange juice
55g or 2 oz blanched and toasted almonds
The rind of 1 orange

Method
Remove the meat from the chicken and cut into strips.

Grate the rind from the oranges, remove the peel and pith and divide into segments.

Save any juice and add it and the extra orange juice to the mayonnaise together with the grated orange rind.

Toast the almonds until nut brown and cut into slivers.

Mix the almonds and the chicken with the mayonnaise, then put into a deep container. Cover and chill.

Just before the meal, turn out the chicken mayonnaise and garnish with slices of orange and watercress.

Jenny's Raspberry Creams

My friend the chef Jenny Beard now runs her own restaurant, Hafod Lodge, at Cwmystwyth near Aberystwyth, with menus mainly in Welsh and food of mainly Welsh origin. I have added a touch of ginger wine to her raspberry creams recipe.

Ingredients (Serves 4 to 6)
55g or 2 oz toasted oatmeal
300ml or half pint of whipped double cream
4 tbs clear honey
1 tbs whisky
2 tbs ginger wine
Half tsp ground ginger
350g or three-quarters lb raspberries
A few toasted cashew nuts

Method
Toast the oatmeal and let it cool.

Combine the oatmeal, cream and honey. Fold in the whisky, ginger wine and ground ginger.

Place the mixture between layers of the raspberries in glass goblets, finishing with the cream mixture. Serve very chilled, and sprinkle with some toasted cashew nuts.

'After Eight' Roulade

Ingredients

5 eggs
170g or 6 oz caster sugar
170g or 6 oz plain dark chocolate
2 tbs hot water
Icing sugar for dusting
300 ml or half a pint double cream
Dash of oil of peppermint, or peppermint essence
Box of 'After Eight' mints

Method

First prepare a paper case. Cut a piece of greaseproof paper 2 inches or 5cm larger all round than a 9 by 13 inch (23 by 33cm) swiss roll tin. Make a diagonal cut into the corners. Put the paper in the tin and crease the bottom edges. Overlap the corners to make a case above the rim of the tin. Secure the corners with paper clips. Brush lightly but evenly with oil and dust lightly with flour.

Separate the eggs. Add the caster sugar to the yolks and beat until light and creamy.

Break the chocolate into a saucepan and melt over a very gentle heat, then add the hot water and stir until well blended and smooth.

Stir the melted chocolate into the creamed egg yolks.

Beat the egg whites until they form soft peaks. With a metal spoon lightly fold into the chocolate mixture, then pour into the prepared tin.

Bake for 15 to 20 minutes in an oven at 350°F, 180°C or gas mark 4.

Remove from the oven, cover immediately with a clean tea towel. Leave until quite cold.

Turn the roulade onto a piece of greaseproof paper well dusted with icing sugar, then remove the paper case. Spread the whipped cream to which has been added a dash of oil of peppermint, or two drops of peppermint essence. Roll up and decorate with piped cream and 'After Eights' halved in triangles.

'Irish Coffee' Roulade variation

Follow the above recipe, but omit the peppermint essence and add coffee essence to the egg yolk and sugar cream. Also add a dessertspoon of coffee powder and two teaspoons of Tia Maria liqueur to the whipped cream filling. Use triangles of 'Irish Coffee' thins to decorate.

Burton Court Brown Bread

Ingredients (Makes 2 x 1 lb loaves, or 1 x 2 lb loaf)

25g or 1 oz fresh yeast

55g or 2 oz fine bran

400g or 14 oz stoneground flour

225g or 8 oz granary flour

Half tsp salt

1 dsp honey

1 and a half tbs oil, or 25g or 1 oz lard

450ml or three-quarters pint hand hot water,

 or 300ml or half a pint skimmed milk and 150ml

 or a quarter pint water

Appx. 1 tbs sesame seeds, cracked wheat or poppy seeds

Method

Mix yeast with a little of the water. Mix the dry ingredients in a bowl, add the yeast, oil, water and/or milk and honey.

1 minute. Dough hook in an electric mixer, then knead by hand.

8 minutes. Knead (turn, fold, push, crash down). Place in a clean greased bowl. Pat with greased fingers to prevent crust forming. Cover with cling-film.

First rising. Leave 1 hour, or until double in size. Finger dent test at edges. Heat oven to 425°F, 220°C or gas mark 7. Place a steam pan of hot water in the oven.

10 minutes. Knock back (turn, fold, push, crash down). Flatten dough to roughly the width and length of the tin. Place in greased or Pullman tin under a dome covered with a towel.

Second rising. Leave for 1 hour or until raised 1 and a half inches above the tin line. Milk glaze, sprinkle on the sesame seeds, cracked wheat or poppy seeds.

Bake for approximately 40 minutes, turning round after 20 minutes and remove the steam pan. Test for a hollow sound, and if not done then return for another 5 minutes.

Cool on a wire rack.

A friend of some thirty years standing has been the American master baker and food writer Bernard Clayton Jr. He studied every method of bread making, visiting bakeries all over the world before producing his mammoth *The Complete Book of Breads* first published in 1973. He has since produced a revised and expanded edition in 1987, and subsequent books on the breads of France, pastry, and soups and stews and is currently working on an encyclopaedia of American food. To my delight he has included a couple of my recipes in his titles, and has tested the bread recipes in this book.

Burton Court Poppy Seed Plait and Christmas Stollen Bread

This recipe makes 3 poppy seed plaits and one small Christmas stollen loaf, which is best served sliced and buttered. In Germany bakers begin to prepare their stolle de Noël, the Christmas stollen bread, at the start of the festive season. Traditionally this recipe includes schnapps or brandy, almonds, orange and lemon peel, but this is a simplified version and I like to use almond paste.

Ingredients for the milk dough
1.35kg or 3 lbs strong plain flour
3 level tsp salt
55g or 2 oz butter or margarine
30g or 1 oz fresh yeast
300 ml or half a pint lukewarm water
600ml or 1 pint lukewarm milk
2 standard eggs, beaten

2 tbs poppy or sesame seeds

For the Stollen Bread
Quarter of the dough as prepared below
15g or half oz melted butter
1 heaped tsp powdered cinnamon
Half tsp ground ginger
55g or 2 oz whole hazelnuts
1 tbs soft brown sugar
25g or 1 oz chopped flaked almonds
170g or 6 oz ready-made white marzipan
Milk for glazing and a little extra melted butter.

Method
Sift the flour and salt into a bowl. Rub in the fat finely. Blend the yeast with a little water, then stir in the remaining water and milk. Make a well in the centre of the dry ingredients and pour in the yeast mixture and the beaten eggs.

Mix with the hand to form a soft dough, then using a kneading movement, beat well with the hand until the dough is elastic and smooth.

First rising. Cover with greased cling film or a damp towel and leave to rise in a warm place for about 45 minutes, until doubled in bulk. Risen dough will spring back when pressed lightly with a floured finger.

Second rising. Turn risen dough on to a lightly floured surface and knead well. Cut the dough into 4 equal pieces, and then divide 3 of the quarters into 3 equal pieces. Roll the 3 equal pieces from each quarter into equal strips approximately the length of the baking sheet, and plait, so forming 3 plaited loaves. Leave to rise again on greased baking sheets, covered in airtight plastic bags or under a dome in a warm place until doubled in size.

(The remaining dough is for the stollen bread.)

Heat oven to 450°F, 230°C or gas mark 8. Place a steam pan of hot water in the oven.

Brush the loaves lightly with a little beaten egg and sprinkle poppyseeds or sesame seeds, bake in the very hot oven for 20 to 25 minutes until well risen and golden brown, then cool on a wire rack.

Returning to the stollen bread, flatten the prepared dough into an oblong 14 inches by 8 inches.

Brush the melted butter over the surface to within 1 inch of the edges. Mix together the cinnamon, ginger and chopped flaked almonds, whole hazelnuts and the brown sugar and sprinkle over the melted butter. Roll out the marzipan in icing sugar to about 12 inches by 6 inches and place on the top.

Roll up the dough so that it looks like a swiss roll, starting with a short end, and tuck the ends underneath. Put the roll into a greased 2 lb tin or Pullman tin, and make four diagonal cuts a quarter of an inch deep on top of the roll, using a sharp knife.

Cover and leave under a dome shape for 20 minutes, or until well risen. Brush with milk to glaze.

Cook in a moderately hot oven, 400°F, 200°C or gas mark 6, for 30 to 40 minutes until golden brown. Remove from the oven and brush all over with a little melted butter.

If you wish you can brush it with a glaze made from 115g or 4 oz sifted icing sugar, 2 tablespoons water, a squeeze of lemon juice and quarter teaspoon vanilla essence, and decorate it with cherries and chopped nuts.

After Dinner Savouries

'Strange to see how a good dinner and feasting reconciles everybody.' Samuel Pepys.

Escoffier scoffs slightly at the use of savouries after a meal saying that it goes against the rules of gastronomy and has no right to be included in a classical menu. However, he then lists some 43 ideas!

Personally, I believe that savouries are back in fashion and that they represent a neat and exciting way to finish that 'special menu' and are a pleasant alternative to serving mounds of cheese.

An infinite variety can be made from a basic béchamel sauce made from 1 and half oz or 45g butter, the same weight of flour, 15 fl oz or 450ml of milk, 1 bay leaf, a parsley stalk, a sprig of thyme and 1 slice of onion.

Method

Heat the milk with the bay leaf, parsley, thyme and onion. Cool and strain off the herbs and onion.

Melt the butter in a heavy saucepan. Add the flour and stir over a gentle heat for 1 minute. Draw the heat off the pan and gradually add the strained milk. Mix well or whisk until smooth.

Return the sauce to the heat and stir or whisk continually until boiling. Simmer for 2 or 3 minutes and season with salt and pepper to taste.

The bases can be anything from deep fried rounds or squares, filo pastry baskets, puff pastry rounds, medium sized vol-au-vents, bread lined pastry cases or barquettes. They can be pre-cooked in an oven at 400°F, 200°C or gas mark 6 for 10 minutes, and cooled.

Nearly any kind can be presented, and it is fun and exciting to create your own ideas. Some to start you off are listed below, and are just added to the basic three-quarters pint of béchamel sauce.

Serve on small side plates.

Toasted Walnut and Stilton Savoury

Chop and toast 2 oz or 55 g freshly shelled walnuts, reserving half a whole walnut for each case as a final garnish. Add 5 oz or 140 g crumbled stilton cheese, 1 dsp finely chopped parsley, half a tsp ready-made mustard and black pepper. Add to the basic sauce and melt the cheese. Do not boil.

Just before serving, place under the grill to slightly brown, then garnish with the half walnut and a spring of parsley. (Port wine can be added to the sauce if you wish.)

Wensleydale and Apple Savoury

To the basic sauce add 5 oz or 140 g wensleydale or cheshire cheese, add a diced and finely chopped eating apple, including its skin. For a garnish, spread a few strands of coarsely grated red leicester cheese before melting under the grill. Finally garnish with parsley and a few sliced sautéd button mushrooms.

Tuna and Anchovy Savoury

To the basic sauce add 4 oz or 115g flaked tuna and 1 tsp anchovy essence. Lightly grill on a base and garnish with circles of anchovy fillets and black olives. Serve immediately.

Double Gloucester & Pickle Savoury

To the basic sauce add 5 oz or 140g double gloucester melted down, with 1 tbs pickle (Branstons or similar), and also add a few drops of Worcestershire sauce. Toast under the grill and garnish with a few strips of tomato.

Other savouries

Scrambled Kipper

Prepare the required amount of medium vol-au-vent cases. Lightly scramble 3 or 4 eggs with a tablespoon of cream. Add flaked warmed tinned kipper fillets, and then pile into the cases and dust with sesame seeds. Finally garnish with a sprig of parsley.

Devils on Horseback

Another traditional savoury. This recipe makes 8 savouries, and allow 2 per person. Stone 16 large cooked pitted prunes. Cut 8 long rashers of streaky bacon into halves, and stretch and wrap them around the prunes, securing with a cocktail stick. Cook under the grill until the bacon is crisp and brown, turning once or twice. Serve on pieces of fried bread or toast fingers, dusted with paprika.

Kitchener Tartlets

Fill the tartlet cases with poached flaked smoked haddock in a curry flavoured cheese mornay sauce. Heat under the grill, then decorate with a ring of gherkin or olives. A variation would be to fill filo pastry baskets with the mixture. Filo baskets are made from 4 sheets of filo pastry squares, approximately 5 inches square, well buttered and wrapped around the base of jam jars, and then baked for about 7 to 10 minutes at 200°C, 400°F or gas mark 6 until brown. Leave to cool on the jars before removing the baskets. (Filo pastry is increasingly versatile and most supermarkets now stock it.)

Bengal Savouries

Mix 4 oz or 115g finely cubed cooked lean ham, 2 tbs thick cream, 2 tbs mango chutney, finely chopped, and 2 tbs grated cheese. Pile into vol-au-vent cases or filo pastry baskets. Warm up well and garnish with parsley and tomato.

Escoffier's Camembert Fritters

Cut camembert into long diamond shapes, discarding the rind. Sprinkle with cayenne pepper and pass twice through egg and breadcrumbs. Deep fry in hot fat at the last moment. Drain and serve on a lettuce leaf.

William Verrall's Eighteenth Century Savoury

Cut some strips of bread the length of anchovy fillets. Fry them in oil or butter and drain. Cover the anchovy fillets liberally with fresh grated parmesan cheese and place on the fried bread strips and heat gently in the oven. Squeeze a little lemon juice over them and place on a crisp lettuce leaf. Garnish with parsley.

... and finally ...

The sixteenth century Sheldon Tapestries hang in a dimly lit corner of London's Victoria and Albert Museum. Most unusually for their period they depict a map of Herefordshire, Worcesterhsire and parts of Shropshire and Warwickshire. Sadly, there is an enigmatic repair where Burton Court should be.

Perhaps the recipes in this book will help keep Burton Court more firmly in people's minds in future.

Certainly English food has gained more renown than when Prince Francesco Caraccioli is reputed to have said 'In England there are sixty different religions, but only one sauce.'

List of Specialist Suppliers

For Pullman bread pans and baking trays a price list and catalogue can be obtained from Pullman Pans Ltd., Eastfield Industrial Estate, Penicuik, Nr. Edinburgh. EH26 8HA. (Tel: 0968 78386)

Fox's smoked salt can be obtained from Fox's Spices marketing Ltd., Aston Cantlow Road, Wilmcote, Stratford-on-Avon, Warwickshire CV37 9XN. (Tel: 0789 266420)

Dried marigold petals and orris root powder are available from Culpeppers, 21 Bruton Street, London W1X 7DA (Tel: 071 629 4559)

Bibliography

The Form of Cury Facsimile reprint of the Rev. Richard Warner's book *Antiquitates Culinaire*, 1791. Prospect Books. 1983

Boke of Nurture by John Russell, 1460, Ed. J. Furnivall (Ed), published with:

Early English Meals and Manners Early English Text Society 1868

The Good Huswifes Jewell by Thomas Dawson, London 1596. Facsimile 1977

Leith's Cookery School by Prue Leith. Macdonalds 1985

The Compleat Angler by Izaak Walton. OUP 1935 and World Classics Paperback 1988

The Complete Servant by Samuel and Sarah Adams. Southover Press 1989

The London Art of Cookery by John Farley 1783. Southover Press, 1988

The Complete Book of Breads by Bernard Clayton Jnr. Simon & Schuster 1973

The Complete Book of Pastry by Bernard Clayton Jnr. Simon & Schuster 1981

The Gentle Art of Cookery by Mrs C.F. Leyel and Miss Olga Hartley. Graham Watson ltd 1925

William Verrall's Cookery Book 1759. Southover Press 1988

The Art of Cookery made Plain and Easy by Hannah Glasse 1747. Prospect Books 1983

The Experienced English Housekeeper by Elizabeth Raffald 1769. Paul Minet reprints 1972

Food & Cooking in Medieval Britain. History & Recipes by Maggie Black. Historic Buildings and Monuments Commission for England 1985

The Best of Eliza Acton. Penguin Books 1974

Lady Fettiplace's Receipt Book by Hillary Spurling. Penguin Books 1987

Good Food and Wine by André Simon. Collins 1952

The Art of British Cooking by Theodora Fitzgibbon. Phoenix House 1965

Good things in England by Florence White. Jonathan Cape 1968

Food in History by Reay Tannahill. Penguin Books 1973

Seven Hundred Years of English Cookery by Maxine McKendry. Weidenfeld & Nicholson 1973

The Compleat Housewife by Eliza Smith, 1727. Facsimile copy, Arlow House Publishing 1983

The Art of British Cooking by Theodora Fitzgibbon. Phoenix House 1965

The Sheldon Tapestry Weavers & their Work by E.A.B. Barnard and A.J.B. Wace. The Society of Antiquaries of London 1928

Other books from Logaston Press

Is it still raining in Aberfan?
Photographed by Martin Dunkerton and written by Melanie Doel, this book records the history and life of the Merthyr Vale colliery and its people from its inception to its recent closure. Much of the text is stories told by miners, their wives and family, including some of those caught in the disaster of 1966. Over 110 photographs. ISBN 0 9510242 9 9

Alfred Watkins - A Herefordshire Man
By Ron Shoesmith, Hereford city's archaeologist, this book chronicles the life of the author of *The Old Straight Track* the book which gave birth to Ley Lines. Watkins dabbled in much, inventing the first exposure meter and the book includes over 45 of his own photographs. ISBN 0 9510242 7 2

Walks & More
By Andrew Johnson & Stephen Punter this is an illustrated guide book to an area from Llandrindod and Builth Wells to the River Severn, from Ross and Ledbury in the south to Stourport and Ludlow in the north. With 80 circular walks, chapters on history, agriculture, folkore, cider, beer and art and literature, and a gazetteer to over 150 towns and villages. ISBN 0 9510242 6 4

The Humble-Bee, Its Life History and How to Domesticate It
By F.W.L. Sladen. Originally published in 1912 and still a classic work, Sladen enthusiastically weaves together the strands of a simple story of natural history and those of profound scholarship in a way accessible to young and old. This edition includes a copy of Sladen's original hand-written monograph of 1892. ISBN 0 9510242 3 X

The Happy Farmers
By Sheila Wenham who first met Mary at a bull sale in Hereford in 1944, since when they farmed together. But the book is much more than a simple farming story. It's a story about a successful partnership between two women in what is still essentially a man's world, and they became top breeders of Kerry Hill sheep, of Hereford cattle and of Welsh Mountain ponies. It's a book full of local character, life and photographs. ISBN 0 9510242 4 8

Aspects of Herefordshire
By Andrew Johnson & Stephen Punter the book covers many aspects of Herefordshire—the county town and the market towns, agriculture, cider, Hereford cattle, Ryeland sheep, the oak, the River Wye, dragons, architecture, romanesque carvings, detached belltowers, Croft Ambrey, Offa's Dyke, the Mortimers, the Hospitallers, Sir John Oldcastle, Nell Gwyn and Colonel John Birch. With specially commissioned illustrations. ISBN 0 9510242 1 3

Also: **Aspects of Worcestershire** by Andrew Johnson & Stephen Punter
       Ludford Bridge & Mortimer's Cross by Geoffrey Hodges
       Walks in Southern Powys & the Borders by Andrew Johnson